How to Write a Great Script with Final Draft 9

Wallace Wang

DEDICATION

To all aspiring screenwriters who want to use Final Draft 9 to help them convert their great ideas into even greater screenplays that all of us can enjoy as movies in the near future.

CONTENTS

INTRODUCTION

Most computer book tutorials get it wrong. Flip open any computer book and you'll typically see a thick tome crammed with information about every possible feature of a program in exhaustive detail. Such comprehensive detail makes most computer books about as exciting to read as a dictionary.

Nobody really wants to learn how to use any particular program. What people really want to learn is how to get specific results from using a particular program.

Chances are good that your goal in life isn't to learn how to use Final Draft 9. Instead, you probably really want to learn how to write the best screenplay possible with the least amount of hassle. To achieve that goal, you want to use Final Draft 9 as a tool to achieve your dream of writing a screenplay that you can sell.

That's why this book won't teach you how to become a Final Draft 9 expert. What this book will teach you is how to plan, organize, and write a screenplay using Final Draft 9 as a tool to make your task easier.

Notice the huge difference?

You want to be a screenwriter, not a Final Draft 9 computer expert. So this book will teach you how to use Final Draft 9 to make you a more effective screenwriter.

Not only will you learn how to use Final Draft's most common features, but you'll also learn why to use them and how they can help you organize and write a more effective screenplay. To use Final Draft most effectively, you need to know how to develop a story. Having a great screenwriting program like Final Draft 9 is fine, but if you don't know what to write, then you won't be able to take advantage of Final Draft 9's writing, formatting, and editing features.

Although Final Draft works as an excellent screenplay formatting word processor, that's actually the last feature you want to use. Where most people go wrong is that they focus first on writing their screenplay without knowing what to write or taking time to organize their ideas before they write.

Think of screenwriting like planning a vacation. You could just show up at the airport and hop on any plane, but chances are good it won't take you where you want to go. Likewise if you start writing a script without any planning, you'll likely waste time writing an rambling and incoherent screenplay. At this point, formatting your screenplay perfectly means nothing if it's not structured to tell a compelling story in the first place.

So this book will teach you how to write screenplays using Final Draft 9 as a tool. If you want to learn how to become a better screenwriter and use Final Draft 9 to help you achieve your ultimate goal of selling a screenplay, then turn to the first chapter and let's get your award-winning screenplay started!

Wallace Wang

1 GETTING IDEAS

Before you can even start writing a screenplay, you need an idea. Start by summarizing your story in one sentence. Your story idea should contain four elements:

- A hero with a seemingly impossible goal
- A problem that creates a dilemma for the hero
- A deadline
- The threat of death

All stories are about somebody even if your hero is a robot ("WALL-E"), a pig ("Babe"), or a car ("Cars"). Whether your hero is a person or not, your hero represents the focus of your story. In every story, audiences need someone they can root for because your hero is pursuing a seemingly impossible goal. The more difficult the goal, the greater our respect for the hero in pursuing that goal. Climbing a flight of stairs isn't an interesting goal because it's fairly easy to achieve. Climbing Mount Everest is an interesting goal because its difficulty makes it less likely to achieve.

Besides an impossible goal, every audience stays glued to their seats when a story creates problems that block the hero from a goal. Once we know that a hero wants something important, we want to know how she will get it. If a hero wants a goal and immediately achieves it, that's boring. Audiences really want to see a hero struggle to achieve a worthwhile goal. That struggle makes us fear that the hero might fail, but also keeps us wanting to know if the hero might overcome all problems and achieve the goal anyway.

Problems define every story. Without problems to create conflict, there is no story. Imagine a story about a man who goes shopping. There's no worthwhile goal and there's no conflict. As a result, there's no story.

Now let's see what happens when we add a problem. A man goes shopping and suddenly spots the woman of his dreams. The problem is how can he get to know her? With a goal and a problem blocking that goal, the story suddenly becomes more interesting.

To crank up the interest, let's add a deadline. A man goes shopping, spots the woman of his dreams, and has to get to know her before she leaves the shopping mall where he might never see her again. Notice that this is far more interesting than just a story about a man going shopping. Just by adding a goal and a deadline cranks up the tension and suspense.

To really ratchet up the tension, let's add the threat of death. If the hero fails to achieve his goal, he'll either experience physical death or emotional death. A physical death means the hero could die, which is the common threat used in action/thrillers like "The Expendables" and every James Bond movie. An emotional death means that the hero may live, but may miss out on a once in a lifetime opportunity. In every romantic comedy, the hero risks an emotional death if he or she doesn't find true love.

Whether you have a physical or emotional death, the threat of death adds extra urgency to any story. Not only must the hero pursue a seemingly impossible goal, but she must also face a deadline where failure could mean physical or emotional death.

Suppose a man goes shopping, spots the woman of his dreams,

talks to her for a while to realize she's the one for him, then loses sight of her in the largest shopping mall in America. Now he has to find her before she leaves and he might never see her again. To add the threat of emotional death, imagine this man is already engaged to be married but suddenly realizes that he's going to marry the wrong woman. If he doesn't find the woman of his dreams, he'll not only lose her, but also suffer from an emotional death by getting stuck in an unhappy marriage.

Does the threat of an emotional death, combined with a deadline and a goal make this simple story dramatically more interesting than a story about a guy who goes shopping?

Now that you know that every story needs a hero, a goal, obstacles, a deadline, and the threat of death, study the summaries of the following movies:

- "Alien" — The crew of a spaceship must find a way to defeat a carnivorous alien that's killing them one by one.
- "Titanic" — A woman finally finds love, but it's on the maiden voyage of the Titanic.
- "The Hunger Games" — A teenage girl, living in a dystopian future world, must survive a reality TV show where only one person can win by killing the other contestants.
- "E.T." — A boy must help a stranded alien get back to a spaceship before the authorities can capture it.
- "Back to the Future" — A teenager goes back in time and must help his mother and father meet to make sure he'll be born in the future.

If you can summarize your story in a single sentence that describes a hero, a goal, problems, a deadline, and the threat of death, you'll likely create a great idea for a story. If you can't do that, chances are good that your story isn't quite defined in your mind yet.

It's easier to refine and modify your story idea now when it's just one sentence rather than wait until you've written 120 pages of a script that isn't interesting or coherent. Once you create an exciting, one sentence summary of your story, you'll be eager to start writing. However, if your story summary is vague and uninteresting, you won't know how to start or what to write next.

Novelists can often jump right into writing their story because novels allow room to expand ideas and go off on tangents. As a result, novels can afford a more rambling story telling style with less planning ahead of time.

Screenplays, on the other hand, must stay tightly focused with far less room for exploration. You only have 120 pages where every single page must contribute to your story. Study great movies and you'll find that every scene works together to tell a coherent tale. Watch bad movies and you'll find that scenes don't always support each other, tell the same story, or even complete the ideas they initially set up. That creates a less focused, coherent story, which is why some movies tend to "drag" despite endless amounts of special effects, gunfire, and explosions.

Creating Your Story Idea

The four elements of a story idea sentence include:

- A hero with a goal
- Problems that block the hero from the goal
- A deadline
- The threat of death

Start with any of these four elements. For example, you might want to write a story about a young woman who wants to find love. So you could write:

A young woman wants to find love.

Once you know what goal your hero wants to achieve, you can expand on your idea by adding problems. For a woman to find love, some possible problems might be:

- She's already married or engaged to someone else ("Titanic")
- Her true love doesn't even like her ("The Proposal")
- Her family disapproves of her behavior ("Moonstruck")
- Her true love is married (or going to marry) somebody else ("Four Weddings and a Funeral")
- Her true love lives in another city ("Sleepless in Seattle")
- Her true love belongs to a different social class ("Grease")
- Her true love is another species ("Avatar" and "Twilight")
- Her true love is being forced to kill her ("The Hunger Games")

Don't worry about choosing the "right" problem. At this point, you just want to get as many possible ideas down.

Once you've come up with several problems that could keep your hero from her seemingly impossible goal, think of a deadline that will speed up your story such as:

- Her true love is on a doomed ocean liner ("Titanic")
- Her wedding date to another man is coming up ("Sleepless in Seattle")
- Her true love is getting married to another woman ("Four Weddings and a Funeral")
- Her true love is dying ("The Hunger Games")

Again, think up different deadlines that force your story to speed up to a final conclusion. Just like your list of problems, your list of deadlines may not be used in your final story, but it's important to get as many ideas down as possible so you can choose the best ones to keep.

Finally, think of how your hero could suffer a physical or emotional death by failing to achieve the seemingly impossible goal. If the hero risks physical death, the hero's loved ones typically also risk physical death. In "Avatar," not only does the hero risk getting killed, but if he fails to succeed, an entire species of natives and their planet risks getting wiped out as well.

If the hero risks emotional death, the hero's loved ones typically risk emotional death as well. In "Napoleon Dynamite," Napoleon risks looking foolish performing on stage to help his friend, but if he fails, his friend will also lose the school election. In "Footloose," the hero stands up for dancing. If he fails, he'll look foolish, but all his friends will suffer from not being able to enjoy dancing either.

For your story, decide if your hero risks a physical death or an emotional death. Whatever kind of death your hero risks, that's the same type of death your hero's loved ones must also face.

Exercise #1: Preparing Your Computer

When it comes to ideas, write everything down so you don't lose them. More importantly, if you write anything down, make sure you can find it again. A written idea that you lose is just as worthless as an idea you never wrote down in the first place.

You could write ideas anywhere just as long as you can find it again. However, it's probably easier if you store ideas on your computer. Before you store anything important on your computer, make sure you automatically backup your hard drive regularly. The last thing you want to do is write the greatest screenplay in the world — only to have your hard drive fail and wipe out your only copy.

Without getting bogged down in the technical details, you need to backup every important file on your computer in two ways:

- On an external hard disk
- Over the Internet

First, you need an external hard disk that connects to your computer through a cable. Next, you need an automatic backup program. If you're using a Macintosh, you can use a feature called

Time Machine. If you're using Windows, you can use a feature called Windows Backup. Both free programs make a copy of your files and automatically store them on your external hard disk. Now if something happens to your computer for any reason, you can plug your external hard disk into another computer and retrieve all of your data.

Of course, if your home or office burns down, it will likely wipe out your computer and your external hard disk as well. That's why you need to backup your data to an offsite location, which basically stores your file on another computer over the Internet. Now if something wipes out your computer and your external hard disk at the same time, you can still retrieve your files off the Internet using any computer from anywhere in the world.

Some popular Internet storage services include:

- OneDrive
- iCloud
- DropBox
- Carbonite
- Mozy

Just search on the Internet for "online storage" and you'll find plenty of options. Online storage services typically charge a monthly fee, but to entice customers, they often offer a limited amount of free storage space. The idea is that once you start using their online service, you'll eventually exceed the free storage space limit and will start paying a monthly fee. Until you exceed that free storage limit, these services won't cost anything.

So before doing anything else, make sure you have both an external hard disk and an online storage service where you can store your crucial files. Once you have both backup storage solutions in place, you'll be ready to start writing down your screenplay ideas without ever worrying about losing them due to computer problems.

For additional protection, Final Draft can automatically back up your files periodically (such as every 15 minutes) and store them in a separate folder. This will protect you if you lose your original file, but will not protect you if your computer's hard disk fails. (To protect you if your hard disk fails, you need an external hard disk, and to protect you if you lose both your computer and your external hard disk, you need to backup your files over the Internet.)

To modify Final Draft's automatic backup feature on a Macintosh, follow these steps:

1. Click the **Final Draft 9** menu and choose **Preferences**. A Preferences window appears.
2. Click the **Auto-Save/Backup** tab as shown in Figure 1-1.

Figure 1-1. The Preferences window lets you customize Final Draft's automatic backup feature (Macintosh).

To modify Final Draft's automatic backup feature on Windows, follow these steps:

1. Click the **Tools** tab and click the **Options** icon. An Options window appears.
2. Click the **General** tab as shown in Figure 1-2.

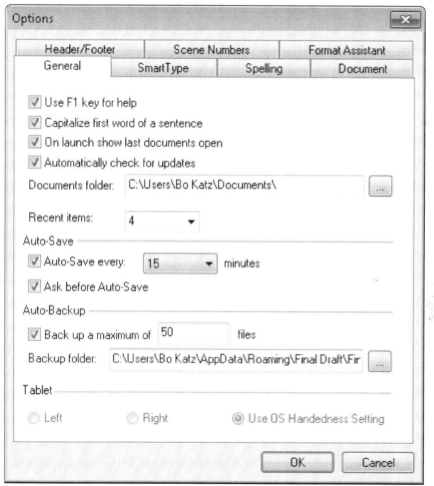

Figure 1-2. The Options window lets you customize Final Draft's automatic backup feature (Windows).

The four automatic backup options you can modify include:

- **Auto-Save every __ minutes** — This lets you specify how often Final Draft saves your file. If this time limit is too low, Final Draft may interrupt your writing to save a backup, which could be annoying. If this time limit is too high, you risk losing your most recent changes if you lose your original file.
- **Ask before Auto-Save** — This displays a dialog box asking you to verify if you really want Final Draft to save a backup of your file. Clear this check box or else you may get annoyed as Final Draft keeps pestering you every 15 minutes or so to save your file. Generally, you want Final Draft to save your file automatically and not interrupt you each time.
- **Backup folder count/Back up a maximum of __ files** — This defines how many backup copies you want to keep. A lower number means fewer backup files to fill your hard disk, but also means you risk not being able to recover older versions of your file. A higher number means more backup files that can clutter your hard disk, but gives you the ability to recover older versions of your file.

With the Macintosh, you can click the **Select New Folder** button to define where you want Final Draft to store your backup files.

With Windows, you can click on the … button to open a Browse For Folder dialog box where you can either click on an existing folder to use, or click a **Make New Folder** button to define a new folder to store your backup files.

For additional protection, you can manually create a backup file of your current screenplay at any time:

- Click the **File** menu and choose **Backup** (Macintosh)
- Click the **File** tab and click the **Backup** icon (Windows)

When you choose the Backup command, Final Draft automatically creates a copy of your current screenplay, using the current file name with the date added. So if you're currently editing a screenplay stored in a file called Rosebud, Final Draft would create a backup file with the date attached such as Rosebud12-15-2015. By creating a backup copy of your file, you can further insure that you'll never lose a screenplay in Final Draft.

Occasionally, you may start editing a screenplay and suddenly realize that everything you changed needs to be wiped out. To completely dump all changes up to the last time you saved your file, you can choose the Revert command:

- Click the **File** menu and choose **Revert** (Macintosh)
- Click the **File** tab and click the **Revert** icon (Windows)

If you saved your Final Draft screenplay, made three changes, then suddenly decided you didn't like any of the changes you just made, choose the Revert command and Final Draft dumps your latest changes and reverts your screenplay back to the last time you saved it.

Just keep in mind that if you saved your Final Draft screenplay, made three changes, and then saved your screenplay again, the Revert command cannot eliminate those last three changes. To reverse or undo any change: you need to choose the Undo command:

- Click the **Edit** menu and choose **Undo** or press Command+Z (Macintosh)
- Click the Edit tab and click the **Undo** icon or press Alt+Backspace (Windows)

With Final Draft's backup features protecting your files, an external hard disk protecting your hard disk from failure, and online storage protecting your entire computer area from disaster, you should never lose a file ever again. Since screenplays often sell for six and seven figures, taking a little time to backup your files can literally be a million dollar investment.

Exercise #2: Storing Your Ideas

You could write and store your ideas in any program, but now you risk separating your notes from your final screenplay. There are two solutions to this problem:

- Store multiple, related files in a single folder
- Store all related information in a single file

Storing multiple files in a single folder lets you use different programs to capture your thoughts. You might use Microsoft Word to jot down your story ideas, but use Final Draft to write your actual screenplay. The drawback with multiple files is the risk of misplacing one or more files.

Storing all information in a single file makes it easy to find the one file that contains everything. The drawback is that you may not want to store everything in a single file.

Let's see how you can try both methods in Final Draft.

Storing ideas in multiple files

You can actually use Final Draft as both a screenplay and a general purpose word processor. That means you can store your actual script in one Final Draft file and your ideas and notes in another Final Draft file.

Normally when you start Final Draft, you'll see a blank window designed for formatting a screenplay. However, when you just want to write down ideas, you don't want Final Draft formatting your notes in script format. To avoid this problem, you'll need to tell Final Draft to create an ordinary file for storing ideas.

To create an ordinary file (not a screenplay) in Final Draft, start Final Draft and then follow these steps:

1. Click the **File** menu and choose **New from Template** (Macintosh) or click the **File** tab and click the **New from**

Template icon (Windows). A New Document window appears.

2. Click **Text Documents** to view a list of different types of document templates you can use as shown in Figure 1-3.

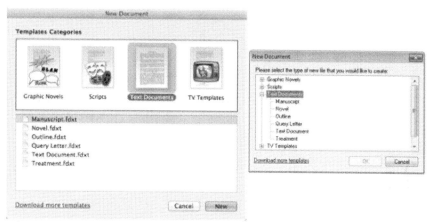

Figure 1-3. The New Document window lets you create an ordinary text document.

3. Click **Text Document** and click **New/OK**. Final Draft displays a blank window with a title of Text Document. At this point, you can type your story idea.

If you store ideas in multiple files, you risk losing track of one or more files. The rest of this book explains how to use Final Draft to store all your ideas (and your screenplay too) in a single file. That way you'll never risk losing track of all your ideas, especially if you make backups regularly.

Storing ideas in a single file

If you store all your story ideas and notes in a single file, you can easily view them while you write your screenplay. Final Draft lets you create and store the following information in a single file:

- A formatted screenplay
- Script notes
- General notes

Your formatted screenplay automatically includes the proper margins and spacing for screenplays, teleplays, and stage plays.

Script notes are meant to store ideas specifically referring to pages of your screenplay. For example, you might jot down ideas in a script note for changing a scene or dialogue on page 24.

General notes are meant to store any ideas related to your screenplay. For example, you might write down links to websites that contain information you need to research. Unlike script notes, general notes aren't necessarily linked to any specific page of your screenplay.

Final Draft displays both Script notes and General notes in a special Navigator window that appears to the right of your screenplay window. That way you can work on your screenplay and view your notes at the same time.

For purposes of writing down a story idea, use a General note. General notes consist of four parts:

- **Name** — This helps you identify the note.
- **Color** — This lets you color code related notes so you can find all related notes quickly.
- **Type** — This lets you define a category type for your notes so you can group related notes together. You can use colors and types to group related notes together.
- **Note Text** — This contains the actual text of your note.

The most crucial part of a General note is the Note Text since that contains the information you want to save and review. A descriptive name can be helpful to identify what type of information that note contains.

Both colors and type can be helpful, especially if you add lots of notes. Some people like using both colors and category types to define their notes, some like just using colors or category types, but many people don't bother identifying their notes at all.

To capture our story idea, we'll create a General note, give it a descriptive name, type in our ideas, and save it. Start Final Draft and follow these steps:

1. Click the **Insert** menu and choose **General Note** (Macintosh) or click the **Insert** tab and click the **General Note** icon (Windows). Final Draft creates a blank General note in the Navigator window that defines the time you created the note as shown in Figure 1-4.
2. Click in the **Name** text box in the Navigator window and type **Story idea** since we're going to store our main story idea here.
3. Click in the **Color** popup menu and choose your favorite color such as Purple or Orange.
4. Click in the **Note Text** box. At this point, you can start typing your story idea.

Now whether you created a separate Text Document to save your story idea or inserted a General Note, define your story idea by describing these four elements:

- Who is your hero and what motivation creates a goal that he wants to achieve?
- What problems block your hero from reaching his goal?
- What deadline is forcing your hero to act?
- What type of death (physical or emotional) threatens your hero?

If you don't have a story idea yet, practice typing in the four story elements for "Moneyball," which is based on the true story of Billy Beane.

- The hero is Billy Beane, the Oakland Athletics' general manager. After losing his best players to free agency, he needs to rebuild his team into a contender.
- Billy Beane has a limited payroll so he can't get the best

players. Instead, he has to use baseball statistics to find inexpensive players that other teams have overlooked. In the meantime, he also has to deal with his own scouts and front office that doubts his strategy will work since it's never been done before.

- Billy Beane has to put together a winning team or risk getting fired at the end of the season.
- Billy Beane risks an emotional death because if his plan fails, he'll be labeled a failure as both a baseball player and a general manager.

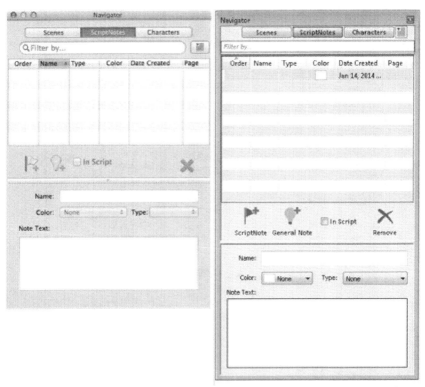

Figure 1-4. The Navigator window displays Script and General Notes.

Exercise #3: Saving a Document

Once you've typed in the four elements of your story idea in either a separate file or in the same file you'll use to write your screenplay, it's time to save your file. When you save a Final Draft file for the first time, you need to define:

- A descriptive name for your file
- Where you want to save the file

You can name your file anything you want, even using spaces in the name such as "My Latest Screenplay". Whatever name you give, make sure that name makes sense to you. A file named "Screenplay58" won't tell you anything if you have dozens of similar files named "Screenplay18" and "Screenplay43" stored on your computer.

Ideally, name your file with the title of your story. Chances are good your final title may change later, so just make up a title that you'll easily remember.

Remember: Once you saved your file once with a descriptive name and location, you won't have to give your file a name or storage location again when you save it.

Whether you stored your story idea in a Text Document or as a General Note, save your file by following these steps:

1. Click the **File** menu and choose **Save** (Macintosh) or click the **File** tab and click the **Save** icon. A Save As dialog box appears.
2. Type a name for your file in the **Save As** (Macintosh) text field or in the **File name** (Windows) text box.
3. Click on a folder to store your file and click the **Save** button. Final Draft keeps your document on the screen even though you saved it.

Tip: You may want to save your file periodically by pressing Command+S (Macintosh) or Control+S (Windows) while you're working, especially if you haven't turned on the AutoSave feature of Final Draft.

Exercise #4: Closing (and Reopening) a Document

Once you've saved your document, you can keep working on it or you can close it. Closing a document keeps Final Draft running so you can create a new document or open an existing one.

- (Macintosh) Click the **File** menu and choose **Close** (or press **Command+W**)
- (Windows) Click the **File** tab and click the **Close** icon.

Note: If you try to close a document that contains changes you haven't saved, Final Draft will ask if you want to save your changes. Unless you're sure you don't want to save your changes, always say Save/Yes.

After you've closed a document, you can open it again. There are two ways to open an existing document:

- Use the Open command
- Use the Open Recent command

The Open command displays an Open dialog box that lets you choose any previously saved Final Draft document.

The Open Recent command only lets you open the most recent documents you last used. If you want to open a document you haven't opened in a long time, you may not be able to use the Open Recent command so you'll have to revert back to the ordinary Open command instead.

To use the ordinary Open command, do the following:

- (Macintosh) Click the **File** menu and choose **Open** (or press Command+O).
- (Windows) Click the **File** tab and click the **Open** icon (or press Ctrl+O).

This displays an Open dialog box that lets you click on the folder and file you want to use.

To use the Open Recent command, do the following:

(Macintosh) Click the **File** menu and choose **Open Recent**. A submenu appears, listing your most recently opened documents. (Windows) Click the **Final Draft** button in the upper left corner of the screen as shown in Figure 1-5. A menu appears, listing all your most recently opened documents.

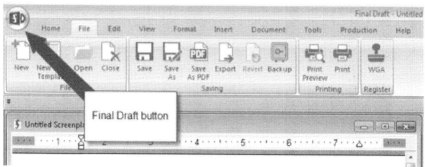

Figure 1-5. The Final Draft button in the Windows version.

To create a new document, do one of the following:

- Click the **File** menu and choose **New**, or press Command+N (Macintosh)
- Click the **File** tab and click the **New** icon, or Ctrl+N (Windows)

Summary

In this chapter, you learned how to create the four parts of a story idea based on an initial idea. You also learned how to create a new file, save it, close it, and open it again. Finally, you learned how to use Final Draft to create an ordinary text document and create a General Note to store ideas.

Here's a quick summary of the different shortcut keys you'll find useful for using Final Draft:

Action	Macintosh keystroke	Windows keystroke
Create a new file	Command+N	Ctrl+N
Create a new file from a template	Command+Shift+N	Ctrl+Shift+N
Open an existing file	Command+O	Ctrl+O
Close a file	Command+W	Ctrl+W
Save a file	Command+S	Ctrl+S

Table 1. Common shortcut keystrokes.

By learning Final Draft gradually, you won't get overwhelmed with its many features. By tackling your screenplay a little bit at a time, you also won't get as easily discouraged. In each succeeding chapter, we'll gradually flesh out the rest of your story idea and learn a different feature of Final Draft until you get to the point of actually being able to write your screenplay.

Tip: If you're using the Windows version of Final Draft and don't like the strange appearance of tabs and icons at the top of the screen, you can switch back to a traditional pull-down menu interface by following these steps:

1. Click the **View** tab.
2. Click the **Switch to Classic View** icon as shown in Figure 1-6.

To switch back to the Ribbon view, click the **View** menu and choose **Switch to Ribbon View**.

Figure 1-6. The Windows version of Final Draft lets you switch between a Ribbon view or a traditional pull-down menu interface.

Finally if you want to exit out of Final Draft, you have several options. If you're using a Macintosh, do one of the following:

- Click the **Final Draft 9** menu and choose **Quit**
- Press Command+Q

If you're using Windows, do one of the following:

- Click the close button (it looks like an X) in the upper right corner of the Final Draft window
- Click the Final Draft button in the upper left corner of the Final Draft window and choose **Exit**

2 PICKING A THEME

Many writing books advise you to write your story and then you'll discover your theme. That might work with a novel, but with a screenplay, every word needs to serve the same purpose so there's no room for wasted text. Rather than write your story and hope that a theme magically appears, it's far better to decide on a theme right from the start. (Don't worry. You can always change your mind just by erasing a few sentences, which is far easier than erasing or heavily modifying several pages of a nearly completed screenplay).

A theme defines your entire story so that every character, scene, and dialogue embraces that idea. In "Avatar," the theme revolves around being one with nature, which is repeated multiple times. When the alien warriors pick a mount, they physically connect with that beast. To live among the aliens, the hero has to merge his body inside an avatar body of an alien. The humans blow up Home Tree, which is where the aliens merge to communicate with the spirit of the planet.

A strong theme guides you by letting you know what works in your story and what doesn't belong. In "Avatar," the theme involves merging with nature, so if the aliens suddenly developed a new technological weapon to defeat the humans, that solution might create glorious explosions and computer-generated special effects, but it would actually dilute the emotional experience of the story when the animals join the aliens to defeat the humans.

Anything that doesn't fit in your theme doesn't belong in your story.

So if you don't know your story's theme, chances are good you'll write a disjointed story. Once you discover your theme (if you ever do), then you'll have to rewrite your story so every part fits into your theme. That could mean wiping out your best scenes and taking out huge chunks of your script. If you don't know your theme ahead of time, you risk wasting time writing scenes and dialogue that will eventually be thrown away.

You don't want to waste time searching for a theme when it's so much easier to come up with a theme in the beginning. From chapter 1, you've already identified the following:

- A hero with a seemingly impossible goal
- Problems that block the hero from the goal
- A deadline
- The threat of physical or emotional death

These four elements represent the bare skeleton of a story. Before you start creating a plot that defines how your hero will pursue an impossible goal with a deadline to avoid physical or emotional death, define your story's theme next.

A story's theme shapes several crucial elements:

- Your hero's fatal flaw, which defines your hero's starting point
- The lesson that your hero needs to learn in order to change, which defines your hero's emotional change
- Your hero's goal
- Your secondary characters' goals
- The villain's goal

Can you see that a theme dramatically shapes any story? If you don't know your theme, you won't know your hero's starting point, how your hero needs to change, what type of goal your hero needs to pursue, or what types of goals your other characters need to pursue. In short, without a theme, your story will likely lack cohesion, consistency, and completion.

Cohesion means that every part of your story supports the other parts. Consistency means that every part of your story supports the same theme. Completion means that your story introduces goals that get fulfilled in the end.

Let's see how this works in"Titanic" where the theme is living your life to its fullest on your terms:

- The hero (Rose) feels trapped heading towards a marriage with a man she doesn't love, which is her starting point.
- Rose needs to learn the theme, which is to live life to its fullest.
- Rose's goal is to find a way to live her life for a change, which she can fulfill by falling in love with Jack, a free-spirited, third class passenger.
- Molly Brown, a women looked down upon for her sudden wealth by the "old money" passengers, also wants to live life under her own terms. Jack, Rose's love interest, already lives life under his own terms.
- Cal, the snobbish and arrogant villain, wants the exact opposite of the theme, which is to oppress Rose.

Do you think it's a coincidence that so many elements in "Titanic" reflect the same theme? If James Cameron had written "Titanic" without knowing the theme, chances are good the various story elements wouldn't have worked together. A story without a guiding theme scatters its focus.

Compare the strong theme of "Titanic" with the movie "Prometheus." In "Prometheus," the lack of a dominant theme causes the different story elements to work in scattered directions. The hero wears a cross necklace that has special significance to her, although we never quite know why. The hero's father died from studying diseases, although we never quite understand why this matters to the hero even though it's somewhat related to the idea of the engineers who created the alien. The starship captain wants to make love with one of her crew members, although we don't know why. The starship captain's father is secretly aboard the ship and wants to talk to the engineers who created the alien so he can become immortal. The engineers represent a race of men who created the human race but later decide to destroy them for an unexplained reason.

"Prometheus" tosses out lots of ideas but never fully explains or completes any of them. As a result of a weak theme, "Prometheus" creates a weak, unsatisfying story.

Every good movie has a dominant theme. In "The Best Exotic Marigold Hotel," the theme is about hope, which is reflected in the goals of all the characters who move from England to a retirement hotel in India. One man wants to reconnect with his male lover from the past. Another woman wants to find a husband. Another man is stuck in a marriage with a stubborn woman who refuses to adapt to India. The hotel owner wants to create a great hotel as a business so he can marry the woman he loves. Everyone either embraces hope or fights to destroy hope. Because "The Best Exotic Marigold Hotel" knows its dominant theme, all the action and characters reflect that same theme to create a coherent and tightly focused story.

It's no mystery that bad movies often lack a dominant theme or fail to focus on a single theme. A dominant theme helps you identify so many different parts of your story that without this guidance, you risk telling different stories in the same screenplay, which will lead to an unsatisfying story.

In "A Clockwork Orange," the theme is about how a man has to choose to be good and can't be forced to be good. The movie (and the book that it was based on) gets its name from the idea that a clockwork orange is something mechanical that appears to be organic. So in "A Clockwork Orange," the hero is a gang member who chooses to do evil. When he's caught, he's tortured into behaving without violence. Then everyone he tormented in his past gets a chance to torture him and he can't fight back. Finally, he nearly kills himself and breaks his mental conditioning so he can finally choose between good and evil once more. Everything revolves around this central idea that a good person is one who voluntarily chooses to be good, so "A Clockwork Orange" tells a coherent, sharply defined story.

You can often see the dominance of a single theme in one movie, and see the complete disregard for that guiding theme in a remake of the same movie. In the 1969 version of "The Planet of the Apes," the central theme is whether humans really are evolved or not. Thus the astronauts find themselves on a planet where humans are hunted and apes are the dominant, intelligent masters. The ultimate irony is that the hero discovers that he's back on Earth where people destroyed the planet in a nuclear war, which makes us question whether humans are really intelligent or not.

Now study the 2001 remake of "The Planet of the Apes" and you'll see that since the original theme has been discarded, the story feels disjointed, especially the disappointing and confusing ending. When the hero gets back to Earth and finds that its entire history has been dominated by apes, that ending simply forces a surprise on us that doesn't support its theme, which is weak and confusing in the first place.

A dominant theme made the 1968 version of "The Planet of the Apes" a classic. The lack of a dominant theme made the 2001 remake of "The Planet of the Apes" a far less satisfying and ultimately forgettable movie. Lots of action and special effects can't make up for the fact that the story lacks a dominant theme.

What makes a classic film? It's usually a well-told story with a dominant theme where the story "proves" the theme:

- "Butch Cassidy and the Sundance Kid" — Failure to adapt to change leads to tragedy.
- "Harold and Maude" — Choose your own life without worrying what others think.

- "Kill Bill" — Revenge is a dish best served cold.
- "It's a Wonderful Life" — The real riches in life are your relationships with others.
- "Citizen Kane" — All the riches and power in the world won't necessarily make you happy.

Great movies not only tell a compelling story, they also "prove" a dominant theme. That's why if you write a story and hope to find a theme, you'll either have to discard large amounts of your writing to refocus it on your theme, or you'll tell an unfocused and uninteresting story. A theme is never optional. A theme defines your entire story like a cup defines the shape of water. Take away a theme and your story goes all over the place, like breaking a cup and spilling water across a table.

Choosing Your Theme

There is no right or wrong theme. There are only stories that use a theme the right way or the wrong way. The right way to use a theme to shape your plot. The wrong way is to try to create an interesting plot without using a theme to define how that plot works.

Once you know your story elements (from Chapter 1), pick a theme. Basically a theme is nothing more than an opinion. Your theme doesn't have to be an earth-shaking insight into humanity. Just make a simple statement and then make sure every element in your story supports that idea.

When you state a theme like you need to choose your own life ("Harold and Maude," "Dead Poet's Society," and "Titanic"), every character's goals, actions, and dialogue subtly supports that idea. Themes are simply beliefs. The more divisive that belief, the better since a divisive theme stirs the emotions of the audience.

What do you strongly believe in? Do you think the world is rigged against women? Then you have the theme for "Thelma and Louise." Do you think it's possible for anyone to achieve their dreams no matter who they are? Then you have the theme for "Babe." Do you believe that there's some hidden conspiracy running the world? Then you have the theme for "The Matrix."

If your strong belief is a positive idea (love conquers all), then you'll likely have a happy ending. If your strong belief is a negative idea (power corrupts), then you'll likely have a tragedy like "The Godfather."

Themes are often a combination of beliefs and explanations of the world around us. In the old days, primitive people told stories to explain something in their world such why the sun rises in the morning or how the leopard got its spots. In today's world, the best stories still explain how our world works using stories with a strong theme.

Think of your favorite movie and chances are good that it explains something about the world:

- "Thelma and Louise" — how women get treated in a male-dominated world.
- "Casablanca" — how you can't isolate yourself from others.
- "Django Unchained" — how blacks were treated under slavery.
- "District 9" — how people treat those who they believe are inferior to them.
- "Midnight in Paris" — how everyone thinks another time period is better than the one they're currently living in.
- "Life of Pi" — how God really does exist in our lives.
- "Moneyball" — how one man can literally change the world of sports by relying on math instead of talent.
- "Brokeback Mountain" — how society's restrictions on gays can affect their relationships.
- "Men in Black" — how the government is really hiding their knowledge of aliens.

Once a movie embraces a strong theme, the entire story sets out to "prove" that theme through the actions of the hero and the villain. The hero embraces the theme while the villain opposes the hero by representing the opposite of that theme.

In "Django Unchained," the hero is a black slave who experiences the horrors of slavery. The villain represents those who profit from slavery. In "Moneyball," the hero learns to question the guessing of scouts and relies on statistics to put together a winning team. The villains are those who oppose his new way of thinking. In "District 9," the hero is a human who learns what it's like to become a despised alien in a human-dominated world. The villains are those who want to keep the aliens oppressed and exploit them.

When you know your story's theme, you know your hero's motivation and the reason for your villain's opposition. Your theme is a combination of a strong belief coupled with an explanation for how the world works. If you want to create a good movie, start with a strong theme.

Exercise #5: Adding Another General Note for Theme

In the previous chapter, you learned how to create a file in Final Draft, save it, and open it again. You also learned how to capture your ideas in a Text Document file or as a single file that you'll eventually use to write your screenplay.

In this exercise, you'll learn how to capture your thoughts on your screenplay's theme in the same file. Remember, the goal is to keep all of your notes and ideas together so you can find and use them again without wasting time tracking everything down.

To open a previously created and saved file, let's use a keystroke shortcut in Final Draft by following these steps:

1. Press Command+O (Macintosh)/Ctrl+O (Windows) in Final Draft. An Open dialog box appears.
2. Click on the file you saved in Exercise #3 from Chapter 1 and then click **Open**. Final Draft displays your document on the screen.

3. Click the **Insert** menu and choose **General Note** (Macintosh) or click the **Insert** tab and click the **General Note** icon (Windows). Final Draft creates a blank General note in the Navigator window.
4. Click in the **Name** text box in the Navigator window and type **Theme** to store your ideas for your story's theme.
5. Click in the **Color** popup menu and choose your favorite color such as Purple or Orange.
6. Click in the **Note Text** box. At this point, you can start typing your story's theme.

Start by typing different beliefs that you feel strongly about. Chances are good that if you feel strongly about a belief, others will too. If you feel a deep emotional connection to a belief, it will be easy for you to apply that theme throughout your writing.

Your belief will subtly change your story. Create a love story and add a theme that love conquers all obstacles, and you might wind up with a story like "Slumdog Millionaire." Start with that same love story, add a theme about forbidden love, and you might wind up with a story like "Brokeback Mountain." Your story idea plus your theme defines your story.

Now focus on what your theme explains about the world. If your explanation focuses on a positive idea, such as "pursuing your dreams makes live worth living," you'll likely have a happy ending like in "Ratatouille." If your explanation focuses on a negative idea, such as "addiction can lead to tragedy," you'll likely have an unhappy ending for your hero like in "Leaving Las Vegas."

Your strong belief defines your story. The way you explain the world through your theme determines the tone of your story whether it will have an upbeat, happy ending or a more somber tragic ending.

In Final Draft, write down pairs of possible themes where each pair contains:

- A strong belief
- An explanation for how the world works

Start by writing the sentence, "I believe…" and fill in the rest.

Then write, "I want to explain…" and fill in the rest.

The theme for "Thelma and Louise" could be written like this:

- I believe we live in a male-dominated world
- I want to explain how women get treated and exploited by men

Remember, there are no wrong themes, beliefs, or explanations. Whatever theme you ultimately choose will shape your story. The best theme is simply the one that you want to use.

Exercise #6: Viewing Notes

By now you've created two General Notes that appear in the Navigator window. One note contains ideas for your story and the other note contains ideas for your theme. Let's see how you can hide and view those notes so you can see them when you need them, and hide them so they don't distract you.

To view and hide notes, follow these steps:

1. Click the **Tools** menu and choose **Hide Navigator** (Macintosh) or click the **Tools** tab and click the **Hide Navigator** icon (Windows). Final Draft hides the Navigator window from view.
2. Click the **Tools** menu and choose Show **Navigator** (Macintosh) or click the **Tools** tab and click the **Show Navigator** icon (Windows). Final Draft shows the Navigator window again.
3. Move the mouse pointer over the Navigator window title bar (the top of the window) and drag the mouse to move the Navigator window on the screen. You may want the

Navigator window to appear next to your document window or somewhere further away.

4. Click the **ScriptNotes** tab in the Navigator window. Final Draft displays all your notes.

5. Click on your Story idea note. The Navigator window displays what you've written for your story idea.

6. Click on your Theme note. The Navigator window now displays what you've written for your theme.

7. Double-click on the **Name** column heading as shown in Figure 2-1. Each time you double-click on any column heading, Final Draft rearranges your notes alphabetically in ascending or descending order so you can quickly find the name of a particular note.

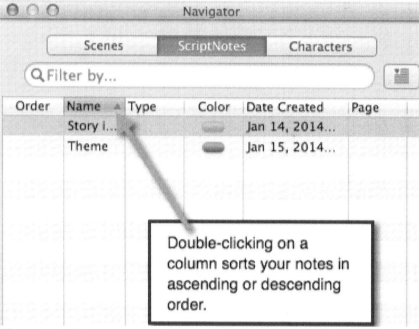

Figure 2-1. You can sort your notes by double-clicking on a column heading.

Remember: You can always delete a General Note by clicking on it and then clicking the **Remove** icon that looks like a big red X.

Summary

In this chapter, you learned how a theme shapes the type of story you tell. You also learned how to create and save another General Note, how to sort your notes, and how to hide and show the Navigator window.

By now you should be comfortable storing ideas for your screenplay in General Notes that you can view at any time. It's a good idea to periodically review your theme to make sure it still makes sense. Sometimes you may start with one theme but once you start writing your screenplay, you realize you're really following a different theme.

It's always okay to change your mind. Of course, it's always easier to change a single sentence than it is to change an entire 120-page screenplay, so it's best to define a theme as early as possible.

Each day when you write your screenplay, look over your ideas for your theme as a reminder. That way anything new you write will stay within that theme. By glancing at your theme periodically, you can keep all elements of your story focused on a single theme.

Save your document by pressing Command+S (Macintosh) or Ctrl+S (Windows). In the next chapter, you'll create a title for your screenplay and learn how to store it in your Final Draft document.

3 THE STORY TITLE

So far you've created a rough outline of your story elements and chose a theme. When you actually start writing your script, you can constantly refer to both your story elements and your theme to make sure they still to your screenplay. By constantly reviewing your story elements and theme each time you work on your screenplay, you can use your story idea and theme as a reminder to help you decide what belongs in your story and what should be discarded.

Another way to guide your story is to come up with a title for your screenplay. When you finally complete and pass out your screenplay for others to review, everyone's going to see the title page first, and the only part of your title page that people care about will be the name of your screenplay.

Think of your screenplay name as an advertisement for your story. If the name is obscure or confusing, it won't matter if the story itself is fantastic. One reason why "The Shawshank Redemption" did poorly in the theaters was because the name confused people. Since they weren't sure what the story was about, they chose to avoid it altogether. Only later when people could see the movie for free on TV did everyone recognize how great "The Shawshank Redemption" had been all this time.

A good name can make your screenplay more appealing. A bad

name will drive people away. You don't want to confuse people; you want to entice them with a hint of what your screenplay offers.

What comes to mind when you see a title like "Gangs of New York," "Saving Private Ryan," and "War of the Worlds"? The titles alone imply action and conflict.

What about titles like "Paranormal Activity," "The Texas Chainsaw Massacre," and "A Nightmare on Elm Street"? Each title clearly implies horror of some kind.

Look at titles like "The 40-Year Old Virgin," "A Fish Called Wanda," and "Ace Ventura, Pet Detective"? These titles imply silliness so they suggest comedy.

Of course, movie titles don't always fit in neat categories. "Harold and Maude" might be a comedy, but "Thelma and Louise" definitely was not a comedy. "The Family" is an action-comedy about a former Mafia boss in the Witness Protection program, but "The Butler" is a historical drama about a White House butler who lives through various Presidents.

Often times you may have a story in mind but won't have a title. Rather than leave your title blank, come up with a temporary or working title. Sometimes you may turn the working title into the final title, but often times any working title is enough to keep your mind focused on your story.

When you finish your screenplay, you can decide if a better title might be more appropriate. As Table 2 demonstrates, many stories began with an awful working title and only got a better title afterwards.

Original Title	Final Title
"3000"	"Pretty Woman"
"When I Grow Up"	"Big"
"Do Androids Dream of Electric Sheep?"	"Blade Runner"

"The Tribal Rites of the New Saturday Night"	"Saturday Night Fever"
"Okavanga"	"Blood Diamond"
"The Cut-Whore Killings"	"Unforgiven"
"East Great Falls High"	"American Pie"
"Ace Ventura Goes to Africa"	"Ace Ventura: When Nature Calls"

Table 2. Before and After titles of famous movies.

Notice that the original title describes the story, but is either too obscure ("Okavanga") or too direct ("The Cut-Whore Killings"). When coming up with a title for your screenplay, experiment until you find one that feels right. Some ways to create a title include:

- A hint
- An emotion
- A contradiction
- A place or time
- An action or event
- A group or organization
- One or more character names

Hints

Since titles advertise what your screenplay is about, you might think that the simplest title would be the obvious one. However, obvious titles don't leave room for imagination, and you want a title that intrigues potential audiences, not give the whole story away. That's why many titles hint at what the story is about.

"The Blind Side" indirectly describes the hero's purpose in football, which is to protect the quarterback's blind side.

"Beauty and the Beast" is about a woman who falls in love with a monster, who is really an enchanted prince held prisoner under a magic spell.

"The Sixth Sense" is about a boy who has a sixth sense that lets him see dead people. Although the title doesn't suggest ghosts of any kind, it does hint at something out of the ordinary.

"Toy Story" is about toys that are actually alive and have adventures of their own. "Toy Story" evokes playful innocence while similar stories with names like "Child's Play" and "The Puppet Master" are actually horror films involving toys.

Think about what your story is about, try to capture the story's plot or emotion, and condense it in as few words as possible.

Emotions

Emotionally charged titles are often best for action, horror, or comedies, but they can work for any story. An emotionally charged title contains an adjective that represents a strong feeling that pervades your overall story.

"Fatal Attraction" condenses the entire story plot in two words. "Attraction" describes the man's lust for a psychopathic woman and "Fatal" describes the consequences when he can't get rid of her as she wrecks his life.

"The Hurt Locker" evokes images of pain and suffering as well as being a common phrase used in the military to describe a painful situation.

"Shakespeare in Love" right away creates an image of a historical love story.

"The Crying Game" evokes images of mourning, pain, and loss.

"The Curious Case of Benjamin Button" right away makes you wonder what's so curious about Benjamin Button. Once you see the movie, you'll see how different his life really is.

Just put an emotionally charged word in a title that describes the general tone of your story and you may have the perfect title.

Contradictions

A title that implies a contradiction can grab someone's attention right away and make them want to know more so they understand what the contradiction means. "Cinderella Man" is about a down and out boxer who gets a chance to fight for the heavyweight championship of the world. Like Cinderella, the hero of "Cinderella Man" represents a rags to riches story.

"Four Weddings and a Funeral" contradicts weddings, which are joyous occasions, with a funeral, which is a somber occasion. This contradiction between weddings and funerals makes us want to know how the story can include two diametrically opposite types of events.

"The Silence of the Lambs" offers an odd contradiction since we don't normally associate lambs as being completely silent. If lambs are silent for some reason, then we assume there must be a reason for this and the title makes us want to find out that reason.

"Kiss of the Spider Woman" contains two different ideas. The word "kiss" and "woman" go together, but rarely do you see them combined with the word "spider," so this title makes us want to know what a spider woman might be.

"Ordinary People" is such a plain title that implies a contradiction because we want to know why we should care about ordinary people.

Combine two seemingly opposite ideas in an intriguing title and that contradiction alone can attract attention. Just make sure that your story actually explains this contradiction in its title because once you set up an audience for a contradiction, you must explain it.

Places or Times

The names of places or specific times are best for historical stories where the location or time holds special significance. Typically the name of a place influences the story. "Chicago" is a musical that takes place during Prohibition in Chicago. Now imagine a movie called "Tokyo" which is really about Godzilla. Even though Godzilla might smash Tokyo, the city isn't that crucial for the story since Godzilla could smash any city and it wouldn't make much of a difference.

"Pearl Harbor" is about the attack on Pearl Harbor, so the emphasis is more on the place than on the characters in the story.

"Born on the Fourth of July" seems trivial until you realize that the Fourth of July holds special significance to Americans as the day of independence. That idea of America plays a large role in the story as the hero fights in Vietnam and comes home paralyzed.

"2012" took advantage of the belief that the world would end in the year 2012. So the whole story is about people trying to survive the apocalypse.

"127 Hours" defines the time a hiker spent with his arm wedged between two rocks where he's forced to choose between staying there and dying, or freeing himself by cutting his arm completely off.

"Midnight in Paris" contains both a time and a place, which makes us wonder what's so special about midnight in Paris.

When titles include time and place, the story absolutely must take place in that time or place or it wouldn't work. "Midnight in Paris" couldn't take place in any other city because only in Paris were all the major historical characters together at one time such as Picasso and Hemingway.

"Lonestar" is a murder mystery, but it has to take place in Texas or else the story wouldn't work as well. As a result, "Lonestar" represents the nickname of Texas.

Likewise, "Apollo 13" couldn't take place anywhere else but in an Apollo space capsule. Since the story is based on a historical event, it could only happen in Apollo 13.

If your story absolutely must occur in a certain place or time, then consider putting the place or time in your title.

Actions or Events

Actions imply what happens in the story. When you see a title like "Kill Bill," that immediately tells you that someone is trying to kill a guy named Bill. The title must capture the dominant action of your story.

"Driving Miss Daisy" is mostly about a chauffeur's job of driving around an old lady named Miss Daisy.

"The March of the Penguins" is a documentary, but it describes the major action of the story, which is the migration of penguins as part of their survival.

"Breaking Away" is about a bunch of kids, treated as second-class citizens, in a college town who dream about breaking away from their life of mediocrity and making something of themselves.

"Django Unchained" implies someone named Django on a rampage after being let loose.

"Mississippi Burning" invokes images of violence that occurred during the racial tensions in the Deep South in the 60s.

What's the dominant action in your story? Identify that action and that can be part of your title.

Groups or Organizations

If the central point of your story involves multiple people, you might focus on the name of that group. Like most stories, "Platoon" is about a hero, but the story revolves around his adventures in a platoon fighting in Vietnam.

"Inglorious Basterds" is about a group of Jewish soldiers killing Nazis while hiding behind enemy lines.

"The Magnificent Seven" is about a group of gunslingers defending a town from bad guys in the old west.

"Dead Poet's Society" is about a group of kids learning what's really important in life through poetry so they form a club called the Dead Poet's Society.

"The Breakfast Club" is about a bunch of kids thrown into detention after school and gradually learn that they are more than their stereotypical beliefs about themselves.

If your story involves a group of people who act together and has a unique name, that might be perfect for your screenplay's title. Generally a group name in a title works best when combined with an emotion ("Inglorious Basterds") or if it's an interesting, non-trivial name ("The Breakfast Club").

A story about kids in school called "High School" would be too plain, but add a little emotion to the title and you get "Fast Times at Ridgemont High," which is far more interesting. Remember, titles work best when they're not too common.

Character Names

Character names in titles work best when the story is about an actual historical or well known figures such as "Lincoln," "Ghandi," "Bonnie and Clyde," "The Last Temptation of Christ," or even "Godzilla" since name recognition alone helps define the story. Tell someone your story is called "Ali" and it's safe to assume it's about the boxer Muhammad Ali and not your neighbor who may also be named Ali.

When your story isn't about a historical figure, character names in titles can be harder to use. "Thelma and Louise" perfectly describes the two women characters, but until you know the story, the title alone might not entice you to see it. Is "Thelma and

Louise" a drama, comedy, action-thriller, or something else? The title alone doesn't give a clue.

Another well-received movie, "Juno," describes the hero, but gives no clue what the story could be about. Only after you know the story does the title finally make sense. For that reason, just putting character names in titles can be less effective than using the other ways of creating a title.

"The Curious Case of Benjamin Button" uses the character name plus an adjective (curious) to pique your own curiosity on what's so special about a guy named Benjamin Button. "Django Unchained" also pairs the character name with an adjective to create greater interest because the title implies that something happens when Django gets unchained.

What if the movie were simply called "Benjamin Button" or "Django"? The names alone don't give a clue what the story might be about, so adding an adjective clarifies the meaning and makes the title more intriguing so we'll want to know more.

Exercise #7: Creating a Title Page

Now that you understand the different ways to create a title, start coming up with titles for your own story. Try as many alternatives as possible such as describing the major event of your story or the dominant action that takes place. You can always change a title later, so feel free to experiment as often as you wish before, during, and after you write your screenplay.

In Final Draft, you can create a title page for your screenplay that's still part of the same file, but separate from your actual script. To create and modify a title page, follow these steps:

1. Click the **Document** menu and choose **Title Page** (Macintosh) or click the **Document** tab and click the **Title Page** icon. A title page window, filled with generic text, appears as shown in Figure 3-1.
2. Highlight the SCRIPT TITLE text area using the mouse or

keyboard, and type your own title.

3. Highlight the "Name of First Writer" text area using the mouse or keyboard, and type your own name.

4. Highlight the "Address" text area in the bottom left corner of the title page using the mouse or keyboard, and type your own address.

5. Highlight the "Phone Number" text area in the bottom left corner of the title page using the mouse or keyboard, and type your own phone number. To make sure someone can contact you, you might also want to type your e-mail address. If someone likes your screenplay and wants to contact you, make sure they have multiple ways of reaching you as quickly as possible.

Figure 3-1. The Title Page window.

Your Title Page actually appears in a separate window that you can move out of the way so you can see your screenplay. To move the Title Page window, do the following:

1. Move the mouse pointer over the title bar of the Title Page window (the top of the window).
2. Drag the mouse (hold down the left mouse button and move the mouse) to move the Title Page window to a new location on the screen.

To close the Title Page window, just click on the close button in the Title Page window:

- Upper left corner of the Title Page window (Macintosh)
- Upper right corner of the Title Page window (Windows)

Every Final Draft screenplay document lets you create a single Title Page that's separate from your actual script. Even if you haven't written a single word of your screenplay yet, creating a title page can give you a feeling of accomplishment. Then take those positive emotions as inspiration to create and complete the rest of your screenplay.

Summary

In this chapter, you learned different ways to create a title for your screenplay. By looking at your screenplay title page periodically, you can use your title to help you stay focused on your main idea. Your title page can also inspire you to complete your screenplay so you can see your title page on the cover of an actual manuscript.

A title can capture your initial idea for a story, but don't be afraid to change it if your story or your feelings about your story change later. The best title is one that captures the essence of your story and piques the reader's curiosity so they'll want to know more.

Save your document by pressing Command+S (Macintosh) or Ctrl+S (Windows). In the next chapter, you'll start defining the characters of your story.

4 THE MAJOR CHARACTERS

Compared to novels, writing a screenplay looks deceptively simple. However, screenwriting can actually be a much harder to tell a story because you have far less room. A typical novel can range from 200 to 1,000 pages, but a typical screenplay is roughly 120 pages. Within those 120 pages, you actually have to tell several stories within your main story:

- Your hero's story that shows how your hero changes
- Your villain's story that shows a horrible goal that a villain is trying to achieve
- Your hero's allies stories that show how your hero changes the lives of those around her
- Your villain's henchmen stories that represents the different ways your villain can oppose the hero

If you study all great movies, you'll find that they often tell multiple stories so multiple characters feel like real people. If you study all bad movies, you'll find that they typically omit the stories of other characters, which makes the overall story feel flat with the other characters serving no role other than to advance the plot for the hero.

Once you realize that a screenplay is more than just telling one story about the hero, you need to keep track of all of these multiple stories and make sure that all of these multiple stories work together based on your theme.

The biggest mistake is to trying to write all story lines simultaneously. This approach often creates incomplete story lines or inconsistent story lines where one story line has nothing in common with any other story line. Incomplete story lines create irrelevant details that simply distract while inconsistent story lines create confusion.

While some screenwriters can keep track of multiple story lines, it's best to focus on one story line at a time. Then add another story line until you've completed all of them. By focusing on one story line at a time, you can complete each one and make sure it supports the same theme as the other story lines.

The keys to every story line is that they support each other, they support the same theme, and their true goals remain mysterious until the end.

In the comedy "Men in Black," the theme is basically about how the government covers up knowledge of aliens. That's not a deep, philosophical belief, but the entire story supports that theme with every action devoted to either dealing with aliens or covering up knowledge of aliens.

Look at how the multiple story lines of "Men in Black" support the theme of government knowledge of aliens. The hero (Will Smith) chases after a suspect and discovers that it's an alien. Now his goal is to discover what's going on until he gradually learns that not only are aliens living among us, but there's a secret government agency that tracks them. Even worse, there's an alien intent on destroying the Earth although Will Smith gradually learns this over time.

No hero can succeed on his own so every hero needs a Mentor. In "Men in Black," the Mentor is Tommy Lee Jones, who also has a goal, which isn't revealed until the end. In this case, Tommy Lee Jones' goal is to train Will Smith as his replacement, so every action that he takes ultimately works towards that goal within the context of the theme about aliens.

The villain in "Men in Black" is a giant bug who takes on the disguise of a farmer. The bug's goal is to find a galaxy, hidden inside a cat's collar, that represents a source of power. The bug threatens to destroy the Earth unless he gets this galaxy.

Notice that each major character is pursuing a different goal that all ties together in the end. Also notice that each goal is mysterious in the beginning but gradually reveals itself over time until we understand everything. Once we understand every goal and see its resolution, the movie is over.

What happens if one of your story lines isn't complete? Then you end up with unanswered questions such as at the end of "Prometheus" where we don't know why the Engineers, who created the human race, also developed the aliens to destroy the human race. With no clear resolution, "Prometheus" leaves us wondering, "That's it?"

What happens if one of your story lines doesn't support the other story lines? Then you wind up with stories that seem to change for no apparent reason. In the James Bond movie, "A View to a Kill," Grace Jones plays one of the villain's henchmen who schemes against James Bond. Then suddenly she's abandoned in a mine by the villain and helps James Bond. Since she doesn't have any goals of her own, her story line simply changes to suit the needs of the plot, creating a disjointed and disappointing movie.

What happens if you only have a story line for your hero but nothing for any other major characters? Then you wind up with a bad movie with stereotypical characters and villains. In "Indiana Jones and the Kingdom of the Crystal Skulls," the villain simply wants to get the crystal skull before Indiana Jones does. Beyond this simple goal, the villain doesn't seem to have any other motivation beyond trying to stop Indiana Jones over and over again like Wiley E. Coyote trying to stop the Road Runner in a Saturday morning cartoon.

Cast of Characters

Every story contains multiple characters. Even a movie like "Cast Away" had to include multiple characters even though the main character was stranded by himself on an island most of the time. In every story, you need the following types of characters:

- Hero — This is the main character who changes over time and takes the most action to achieve a goal. Everything in your story revolves around your hero.
- Villain — This character tries to keep the hero from achieving his or her goal.
- Mentor — This character helps the hero change and become a better person while overcoming a past mistake of his own that can only be resolved through the villain.
- Allies — One or more characters who help the hero, but who also changes for the better through the hero's help. Allies often pursue similar goals as the hero as a way to support and reinforce your story's theme.
- Henchmen — One or more characters who help the villain and who initially confronts the hero until finally getting defeated.

The two most important characters are the hero and the villain. Both the hero and the villain typically pursue mutually exclusive goals so if the hero gets his goal, the villain can never achieve his own goal. Likewise, if the villain gets his goal, the hero can never achieve his own goal.

In every James Bond movie, a villain is trying to destroy the world somehow. If the villain succeeds, he will kill James Bond at the same time. If James Bond succeeds in stopping the villain, then James Bond will kill the villain.

Because the hero and villain have mutually exclusive goals that can only end if one of them dies (physically or emotionally), they absolutely must fight each other.

In "Moonstruck," the hero wants to marry a man, but she's already engaged to marry this man's brother (the villain). If the hero gets what she wants, the villain won't get what he wants. If the villain gets what he wants, the hero won't get what she wants.

By giving your hero and villain mutually exclusive goals, they have no choice but to constantly battle one another until only one emerges victorious. This battle to the death is what creates the main conflict in your story.

Besides pursuing mutually exclusive goals, your hero and villain represent mirror images of each other. In every James Bond movie, James Bond is smart and loaded with technological gadgets. Yet every James Bond villain is also smart and loaded with technological gadgets. Heroes and villains are mirror images of the same character.

It's no secret that in "The Empire Strikes Back," Luke Skywalker (the hero) finds out that Darth Vader (the villain) is his father, or that Luke can use the Force just like Darth Vader.

If your hero wants to pursue a good goal, then your villain wants to pursue an evil goal. So not only is you hero battling your villain because of mutually exclusive goals, but because your hero is also battling the evil version of himself. Your villain is who your hero would be if your hero decided to become evil.

When creating your story, you can start with either your hero or your villain. If you start with your hero, you automatically know that your villain is the evil version of your hero. If you start with your villain, you automatically know that your hero is the good version of your villain. By knowing this, you can create one character to define both your hero and villain.

The Mentor

Your villain is always more powerful than your hero. The only way your hero can even have hope to defeat the villain is through help from other characters, and the most crucial helper is a Mentor.

The Mentor represents the theme of your story and teaches the hero a lesson, which the hero (and the audience) might not fully understand at first. In "The Karate Kid," the hero is a boy who wants to learn karate so he can defend himself from bullies. Since the hero can't learn karate on his own, his Mentor offers to teach him. Initially, the Mentor's exercises seem meaningless but only later does the hero (and the audience) see how they actually taught him how to fight.

In "Up," the hero is an old man who is determined to take his house to a place in the wilderness where he and his wife always dreamed of visiting. In the beginning, the hero's outlook on life is bitter but with the help of a Mentor (a little boy), the hero learns to change and appreciate life.

At the simplest level, the Mentor exists to help the hero. However, on a deeper level, the Mentor also has a goal of her own that she wants to achieve. The Mentor's goal often can be solved only through direct confrontation with the villain and help from the hero.

In the remake of "The Karate Kid," the Mentor is mocked by a rival karate teacher. When the hero defeats the villain (the rival karate teacher's student) it causes the rival teacher's students to flock to the Mentor, thereby helping the Mentor achieve his goal of no longer being shamed by his past.

In "Up," the little boy (Mentor) has no father and feels alone. By helping the hero achieve his goal of embracing life once more, the Mentor also gets the hero to act as a surrogate father figure.

Sometimes the Mentor dies through confronting the villain. In "The Terminator," the hero is a waitress who will give birth to the human resistance leader, and her Mentor is a soldier from the future sent to protect her. To protect her, the Mentor sacrifices himself by shoving a bomb in the Terminator's body, blowing it to pieces but killing himself in the process.

Often times the Mentor is the hero's love interest. In romantic comedies, such as "When Harry Met Sally," both the hero and the Mentor are searching for love. By finally admitting their love for each other, the hero and Mentor both succeed in achieving their goals.

The Mentor is a crucial character who embodies your theme and helps the hero learn that theme in order to defeat the villain and achieve the goal.

Allies

Besides a Mentor, your hero needs the help of one or more allies. These allies help the hero, but the hero also turns around and helps these allies achieve a goal similar to their own. In "Legally Blonde," the hero is a seemingly ditzy blonde from Southern California, trying to attend law school in Harvard so she can win back her boyfriend.

Some of her allies include her hairdresser and some fellow students who are also mocked and dismissed by the other law students. Since the hero is trying to find love, all her allies are also trying to find love.

The hero helps her hairdresser find love by showing her how to get the attention of a handsome UPS deliveryman. The hero also helps her fellow student find love by pretending she liked him to make this student's real love interest jealous so she'll agree to go out with him.

Allies serve two purposes. First, they help the hero. Second, their own goals mirror the hero's goal so it reinforces the theme.

Henchmen

Just as your hero has allies, so does your villain have henchmen. You always want to save the final confrontation between the hero and the villain for the end. Although the hero and villain can battle earlier in your story, the final battle to the death must come at the end. That means the only way your villain can threaten your hero throughout the middle of your story is through his henchmen.

In every James Bond movie, the villain never fights James Bond until the end. Instead, he always sends his various henchmen to attack James Bond. Each time James Bond defeats another henchmen, the villain sends a more powerful henchman to attack him until finally all of them get defeated. That's when the villain personally attacks the hero in the battle to the death.

In "Kill Bill, Volume 1," the hero is trying to kill the female leader of the Japanese organized crime group, who personally beat the living daylights out of the hero in an earlier flashback. Before the villain fights the hero, she first sends her bodyguards to attack the hero. After the hero defeats this army of bodyguards, the villain sends her personal bodyguard to attack the hero.

Although this personal bodyguard causes trouble for the hero, the hero eventually defeats her too. Only then does the villain have no choice but to fight the hero.

In many cases, the villain's henchmen have no goals of their own other than to defeat the hero, such as in "Kill Bill, Volume 1." However, it's better if the henchmen have their own goals so they don't look like mindless puppets.

In "Inglorious Basterds," the main villain is the Jew Hunter, a Nazi who relishes hunting down and killing Jews. Even though he doesn't even meet any of his henchmen, they all work against the hero. First, there's a German officer who detects the British spy, posing as a German soldier. Other than being suspicious, this German officer doesn't have much of a goal of his own.

On the other hand, another henchman, a German sniper, does have a goal of his own, which is to love a French girl who runs a theater. Even though he doesn't plan on interfering with the hero, his pursuit of the French girl does cause problems for the hero just by his presence alone. Because this German sniper has a goal of his own, he seems more like a real person and not just another James Bond-type henchmen who pops up only long enough for James Bond to knock him out.

Exercise #8: Making Up Character Names

Once you understand the types of characters you need in your story, you need to name each character. Although you can choose any name for your characters, choose names that create a visual image of your character. Action heroes typically have short names with hard consonant sounds like John McClane ("Die Hard"), John Rambo ("Rambo"), or Casey Ryback ("Under Siege").

Other types of stories often use longer, more colorful names like Heather Donahue ("The Blair Witch Project"), Sam Baldwin ("Sleepless in Seattle"), and Danny Zuko ("Grease"). Sometimes names are used to identify the ethnicity or nationality of a character like Wikus van de Merwe ("District 9"), Jerry Lundegaard ("Fargo"), and Katniss Everdeen ("The Hunger Games"), which is an odd name to evoke a sense of being in a different world than our own.

Names can also reflect the personality of the character such as Brigadier General Jack D. Ripper ("Dr. Strangelove"), Pussy Galore ("Goldfinger"), and Alfredo Linguini ("Ratatouille"). Even though an audience may not remember the full names of all your characters, the names can help you visualize the type of person that character might be, which will make it easier to write action and dialogue for that character.

One trick to choosing character names is to think of someone you know personally such as a friend or neighbor, or even someone you only know through the news such as a celebrity. Because you already know the personality of certain people, you can apply their names and personality to your characters. Now writing and visualizing what that character says and does will be much easier because you'll already have a visual image of that person in your mind.

To help you find a name for your characters, Final Draft includes a name database. Just type a few letters and Final Draft will show a list of names that match. For example, type in "jo" and Final Draft's name database will show you names like "Joqquin" and "Jovich." Just browsing through different names can often spark your imagination.

To use Final Draft's name database, follow these steps:

1. Click the **Tools** menu and choose **Names Database** (Macintosh) or click the **Tools** tab and click the **Names Database** icon. A Names Database window appears.
2. Click in the Name Prefix text field and type one or more letters such as **jo** and then click the **Look Up** button. Final Draft displays a list of names that match the first characters that you typed as shown in Figure 4-1.
3. Click the **Close** button to make the Names Database window go away.

Whenever you're stuck for a character name, use the Names Database to help you find the right name for each character. Even if you have a minor character, don't give him or her a generic title like Policeman #1. Instead, try to create a more interesting visual image of that generic cop with a name like Policeman Jon or Cashier Martha.

Even the simplest name can create a visual image of that character in ways that a generic title like Policeman #1 or Cashier cannot. When you name a trivial female character Martha, that paints an entirely different image in your mind than if the same female character were named Tiffany or Bambi.

Just make sure that whatever image a name conjures is actually important to your story. If a minor character isn't that important, then it's okay to use a generic title like Policeman #1.

Remember, until your screenplay actually gets filmed, nobody knows what your characters look like, so use creative names to get the right image in the reader's mind.

Finally, make sure your character names are distinct from one another. If your hero is named Sam, you don't want Sam's love interest to be named Samantha. Ideally, make sure your main character names begin with different letters and contain different lengths. If all of your characters have one-syllable names like Sam, Sue, and Sol, that makes it confusing for someone to read in a screenplay. Name those same characters Sam, Jennifer, and Ryan, and suddenly it's far easier for a reader to identify the different characters in your screenplay.

Figure 4-1. The Names Database window.

Exercise #9: Saving Character Information

Once you've chosen names for your major characters, jot down some ideas for that character's personality and save that information as a General Note in Final Draft. That way when you start writing your screenplay, you can refer to your notes about each character so you don't suddenly describe that character as having long blonde hair when earlier it's important that she have short red hair.

Previously when you created a General Note, you chose a color to identify that note. This time you'll not only choose a color, but also a category to help you identify that your group of General Notes as related to your characters.

To save character information based on the character types you need, follow these steps:

1. Click the **Insert** menu and choose **General Notes** (Macintosh) or click the **Insert** tab and click the **General Notes** icon (Windows). Final Draft creates a blank General Note in the Navigator window.
2. Click in the **Name** text box and type **Hero**.
3. Click in the **Color** popup menu and choose a color you haven't used before such as Blue. Whatever color you choose, use this color to identify any General Notes that deal with your characters.
4. Click in the **Type** popup menu and choose **New Type.** A New ScriptNotes Type dialog box appears as shown in Figure 4-2.

Figure 4-2. The ScriptNotes Type dialog box lets you define a category for your notes.

5. Type **Character** (or any descriptive phrase you want to associate with General Notes involving characters) and click **OK**.
6. Click in the **Note Text** box and type the name of your character along with any additional ideas you want to capture at this time.
7. Repeat steps 1-6 for your Villain, Mentor, Allies, and Henchmen so you wind up with five General Notes.

All of these General Notes are just meant to capture your thoughts and keep them handy so you can find and review them again. In most cases, you'll write a lot of information about your characters that you'll never use, but that's okay. The more you know about your different characters, the greater your options for using only the best and most important information.

Summary

In this chapter, you learned about the five different types of characters you need for your screenplay (Hero, Villain, Mentor, Allies, and Henchmen) along with how your hero and villain are mirror images of each other. Once you define your hero, you'll know that your villain is your anti-hero.

Not only is your hero battling against someone with the same intelligence and capabilities that they have, but they're also battling against a villain who has all the advantages on his side. That makes your story much more compelling because your hero has to overcome so many obstacles just for a chance to defeat the villain.

By learning to use Final Draft's Names Database, you can quickly scan through names until you find the right name for each of your characters. Then store your thoughts about each character in General Notes so when you start writing your screenplay in Final Draft, you don't have to hunt around for your ideas about each character.

By color coding and organizing your General Notes with category names, you can help identify all related notes quickly and easily. Already you should see the value of using Final Draft as both a screenplay word processor and a general note capturing and organizing tool.

Save your document by pressing Command+S (Macintosh) or Ctrl+S (Windows). In the next chapter, you'll start defining the individual characters of your story.

5 THE HERO AND THE VILLAIN

Every major character in your story should be pursuing a goal. However, the two most important goals belong to either your hero or your villain.

Most movies are villain-driven, which means the villain's goal initiates the entire story. Think of "Kill Bill," "Under Siege," "Inglorious Basterds," and every James Bond movie. In villain-driven stories, a single, powerful villain starts the story, which forces the hero to fight against the villain.

In villain-driven stories, the villain's goal initiates the story and actively tries to defeat the hero multiple times. Take away the villain and the hero would never have a reason to do anything. Remove the villain (Richard Nixon) from "Frost/Nixon" and there's no conflict. Remove the villain (the power company) from "Erin Brockovich" and there's nothing for the hero to do.

Villain-driven stories introduce the villain early in the story who then attacks the hero (usually through henchmen) multiple times throughout the story. Only when those henchmen fail does the villain finally confront the hero himself for the final climactic showdown.

In villain-driven stories, the villain pursues a huge goal that risks creating Horrible Consequences for innocent people and especially for the hero's loved ones. In "The Lord of the Rings," a relatively defenseless hobbit is trying to keep a powerful wizard from ruling over Middle Earth with an iron fist. If the villain succeeds in achieving his goal, not only will the hero suffer, but all those the hero loves will suffer as well.

In "Erin Brockovich," the hero is trying to bring the villain (the power company) to justice for poisoning innocent people and trying to cover up its actions. If the hero fails, the villain will literally get away with murder.

In super hero stories like "Iron Man 3," the hero not only wants to keep the villain from taking over the world, but also wants to save his girlfriend from getting killed by the villain.

Villain-driven stories force the hero to act. Without the villain pursuing a horrible goal, the hero has no reason to do anything. Only through the intervention of the villain does the hero suddenly have a physical goal to pursue. Take away Darth Vader and who would Luke have to fight against?

Although most stories are villain-driven, some are hero-driven. In a hero-driven story, it doesn't make sense for a single, dominant villain to keep trying to stop the hero. Where villain-driven stories force the hero to stop a villain, hero-driven stories force the hero to battle himself.

In hero-driven stories, a variety of villains pop up to oppose the hero, but there's no single villain coordinating the attacks like Darth Vader commanding stormtroopers to keep attacking Luke and the rebels. Hero-driven stories exist when the hero has a clear goal to pursue right from the start and often needs to travel to different places to pursue that goal.

In "Legally Blonde," the hero's first villain is her ex-boyfriend, who she tries to win back by attending Harvard. Her second villain is the ex-boyfriend's new fiancée, who tries to drive the hero out of school so she can't get near her ex-boyfriend. A third villain is the law professor who tries to pressure the hero for sex. Finally a fourth villain is the prosecuting lawyer in a court case that the hero has to win to save a friend who has been unjustly accused of murder.

If having a single, dominant villain from beginning to end doesn't make sense for your story, then you likely need a hero-driven story. In a hero-driven story, the emphasis is less on fighting others and more on overcoming multiple problems that keep popping up.

In "The King's Speech," the hero's biggest enemy is his own stuttering. First, he tries to find a speech teacher, but none of their methods seem to work. When he does find an unorthodox speech teacher, he struggles to follow his teacher's seemingly bizarre lessons. Just when he's on the verge of success, he has to deal with pressure from others who attempt to discredit the speech teacher because he doesn't have the proper credentials of a typical speech teacher.

None of the villains in "The King's Speech" have a major goal that they're pursuing. Instead, they simply exist to get in the way of the hero. Finally, the hero has to face his greatest enemy, which is his own fear when he must give a speech to rally the nation.

Hero-driven stories are often travel stories. In "About Schmidt," the hero is driving across the country to attend his daughter's wedding. Along the way, he has to deal with a younger worker who will be taking over his job when he retires, his own daughter's in-laws who he doesn't like, and his own loneliness.

At this point, decide if your story fits better as a villain-driven story where a single villain creates a goal for the hero, or as a hero-driven story where the hero already has a clear goal in mind from the start.

If your story relies on outside conflict like "Witness" where the hero must battle corrupt cops, then you have a villain-driven story. If your story relies more on internal conflict like "The King's Speech" or involves your hero pursuing a quest right from the beginning in the complete absence of any villain like "Little Miss

Sunshine", then you have a hero-driven story.

Whether you have a villain-driven story or a hero-driven story, your theme defines both your hero and your villain. In the beginning, your hero represents the opposite of your theme. By the end of your story, your hero has finally changed and succeeded by embracing your theme.

Your villain represents the opposite of your theme, but unlike the hero, the villain never changes and that's why the villain loses.

Exercise #10a: The Villain-Driven Story

In a villain-driven story, your villain defines everything so start by defining your villain. Once you know the type of villain you need, you'll automatically know the type of hero you need who represents the good version of your villain.

(If you're writing a hero-driven story, your villains will likely pop up long enough to cause problems for the hero, but you won't have a dominant villain pursuing a goal, so you can skip to Exercise #10b.)

With a villain-driven story, you need to define the four elements of your villain's pursuit of a goal:

- In the beginning, the villain begins pursuing a big and mysterious goal
- The villain accidentally interferes in the hero's life, forcing the hero to react and interfere with the villain's goal
- The villain tries to eliminate the hero, but fails
- The villain is on the verge of succeeding in his big goal that's finally revealed to the hero

At this point, you just want to sketch out the rough details for how your villain's goal drives your story that causes your hero to react. Don't worry if your ideas aren't complete yet. The point is to capture your initial ideas.

Most importantly, your villain needs to be pursuing a big goal right from the start. Initially, we don't understand this goal. Then we gradually get clues about the goal until the end when we understand the villain's goal. Now the climactic battle between the hero and the villain determines if the villain will finally achieve his goal after all.

In "Alien," the four elements of the villain's goal look like this:

- A strange signal causes a space ship to waken its crew prematurely. Although we don't know this initially, this signal comes from an alien ship, warning others away from the alien (the villain).
- While exploring the signal, the astronauts discover the wreckage of an alien spaceship and a crewman gets an alien stuck on his face.
- The alien starts picking off the crew one by one.
- The hero tries to escape but the alien has stowed away in the escape pod. The alien's goal all along has been to kill everyone and the alien is on the verge of success.

In "The Matrix," the four elements of the villain's goal look like this:

- The villain is trying to crush the human resistance movement that knows the matrix is an artificial world.
- When the human resistance contacts the hero, the villain captures him instead and implants a tracking device in him. When the human resistance fighters yank this tracking device out of the hero, he realizes that his vision of the world isn't what he thought it was.
- As the hero learns about the matrix, the villain captures the resistance leader to crush the resistance for good.
- The villain plans to pry open the secrets from the resistance leader's brain, but the hero rescues him.

By defining the steps that your villain goes through while pursuing a goal, you can gradually define your story bit by bit, like a sculptor slowly stripping away bits of clay to reveal the final form underneath.

If you have a villain-driven story, you'll need to define these four crucial elements of your story:

- What goal is your villain pursuing from the beginning?
- How does your villain interfere in a way that changes your hero's life forever?
- What does the villain do to eliminate the hero?
- How can the villain be on the verge of success?

Let's store the four elements of your villain's story in the General Note describing your villain's name by following these steps:

1. If the Navigator window is not visible, click the **Tools** menu and choose **Show Navigator** (Macintosh) or click the **Tools** tab and click the **Show Navigator** icon.
2. Click the **ScriptNotes** tab at the top of the Navigator window. Final Draft displays all your notes.
3. Click on the Villain General Note and click in the **Note Text** box where you typed the villain's name.
4. Type a paragraph describing the goal that your villain is pursuing from the beginning, but which may be mysterious at first.
5. Type a second paragraph describing how your villain interferes in your hero's life that changes the hero's life forever.
6. Type a third paragraph describing what your villain does to try to wipe out the hero.
7. Type a fourth paragraph explaining how the villain can be on the verge of success.

Since these are just story notes, write more than you think you need, including contradictory ideas. You just want to capture as many ideas as possible so you can review and edit them later.

Exercise #10b: The Hero-Driven Story

Most stories are villain-driven from stories like "The Incredibles" and "Miss Congeniality." However, in some stories the hero begins pursuit of a goal, which drives the entire story. In such hero-driven stories, there is no single dominant villain constantly trying to attack the hero like a James Bond movie.

Instead, the hero doggedly pursues a goal and constantly runs into different and unrelated villains who get in the way. Often the hero pursues a physical goal but winds up achieving a far more important emotional goal in the process.

In "Little Miss Sunshine," the hero is the entire dysfunctional family, but the initial goal is created by a little girl who wants to compete in a beauty pageant called Little Miss Sunshine. That's her physical goal. As we see all the members of this warped family, we gradually understand that the emotional goal is to find happiness. By achieving the physical goal, the hero (the family) can achieve the emotional goal.

The first obstacle the hero runs into is the lack of money, so they decide to drive there in a beat up VW bus. Then the VW bus breaks down and they don't have the money or the time to fix it. Fortunately the problem can be overcome by push starting the VW bus.

Next, the grandfather dies and his body is trapped in a hospital. Unable to get the body released to them, the family simply steals the body and hides it in their car so they can continue driving to the beauty pageant. Along the way, they get stopped by a policeman who almost discovers the dead body of the grandfather in the back.

Finally, they get to the beauty pageant, but they're too late to register. They manage to convince the pageant judge to let the little girl in anyway, and then they realize she's seriously outclassed by the other contestants, so they try to convince her to drop out.

In hero-driven stories, the hero steadily moves towards an initial goal, running into different villains along the way. None of these villains started the story, nor do they have a reason to harass the hero from start to finish.

Instead, they simply pop up when necessary, interfere with the hero, then get overcome until a more powerful villain pops up later to repeat the process all over again.

"Finding Nemo" is another example of a hero-driven story where the hero's initial goal is to rescue his son. First, the hero loses track of the boat that took his son, but he gets help from a forgetful fish who leads him straight to a shark.

The shark doesn't eat him right away, but takes him to a group of sharks all trying to give up eating meat. The shark represents another villain for the hero to overcome. When the hero escapes from the shark, he runs into a blind, carnivorous fish.

The hero escapes from this blind, carnivorous fish and has to deal with the next villain, which are poisonous jellyfish. When the hero overcomes this problem, he gets closer to his goal, but gets eaten by a whale, which represents another villain.

When the hero escapes from the whale, he has to avoid a flock of pigeons who want to eat him. The hero avoids the pigeons and finally makes it to his son, but his son gets flushed down the toilet that leads to the ocean.

The hero eventually reunites with his son, but then some fishermen catch his son. Each time the hero gets closer to the goal, another more powerful villain pops up to get in the way. None of these villains even know about the others, but they all represent the same threat, which involves killing and eating the hero.

The four elements of a hero-driven story include:

- An initial, physical goal that the hero desperately wants to achieve

- The first stepping stone that gets the hero closer to the goal
- A second, more imposing stepping stone that nearly stops the hero from the goal
- An internal conflict that the hero must overcome to achieve the initial goal

Villain-driven stories tend to be more action-oriented while hero-driven stories tend to be more character-oriented.

If you're creating a hero-driven story, store the four elements of your hero's story in the General Note describing your hero's name by following these steps:

1. If the Navigator window is not visible, click the **Tools** menu and choose **Show Navigator** (Macintosh) or click the **Tools** tab and click the **Show Navigator** icon.
2. Click the **ScriptNotes** tab at the top of the Navigator window. Final Draft displays all your notes.
3. Click on the Hero General Note and click in the **Note Text** box where you typed the hero's name.
4. Type a paragraph describing the initial, physical goal that your hero desperately wants to achieve.
5. Type a second paragraph describing the first major obstacle that your hero needs to overcome to move towards the cherished goal.
6. Type a third paragraph describing a second, more imposing stepping stone that nearly stops the hero from achieving the goal.
7. Type a fourth paragraph explaining the internal conflict the hero must overcome to achieve the initial goal.

Exercise #11: The Hero's Change

At this point, you'll have either written down a rough outline for your villain or your hero pursuing a concrete, distinct goal of some kind. In either case, your hero always represents the most important character in your story. Now it's time to flesh out more details of your hero.

Whether you have a villain-driven or a hero-driven story, your hero needs to change over time. How your hero changes depends entirely on your theme:

- In the beginning, the hero is stuck in a dead end life that represents the opposite of the theme
- The hero meets a Mentor, who teaches her a lesson that represents the story's theme
- The hero nearly fails and realizes that her old way of life (the opposite of the theme) no longer works
- The hero changes by embracing the Mentor's Lesson and succeeds

Until you know your theme, you won't know where to start your hero, what your hero needs to learn to change, and ultimately where your hero will wind up after changing. No amount of special effects and pointless action can disguise the lack of a dominant story theme to shape your hero's story.

The theme of "Monsters, Inc." is basically that you can get more out of life by making people happy than by making them unhappy. In the beginning, the hero is the scariest monster who frightens little kids to generate power for the monster world. Although his life seems good, he doesn't even know he's in a dead end.

One day, the hero meets a little girl who isn't afraid of him, but actually likes him. Suddenly he sees that little kids aren't just for scaring, but can be friends and bring joy to his own life as well.

When forced to scare little kids, the hero frightens this little girl, and suddenly feels bad, which makes him realize what a dead end life he really has been living all this time.

The hero suddenly learns that monsters can generate more power by making kids laugh than by making them cry and scream, which helps the hero stop the monsters from scaring kids any more.

The hero changes because of the theme. In "Men in Black," Will Smith starts out not believing in aliens. Along the way, Will Smith (and the audience) learns how aliens really work in the world and how the government hides their existence. Finally, Will Smith helps save the world by defeating the alien villain. By the end, Will Smith is now an expert on dealing with aliens.

Ideally, the audience doesn't even realize there's even a theme guiding the story, but if the story is coherent, the audience will absorb the theme through their enjoyment of seeing how a tightly focused story evolves over time.

Knowing your theme, you can outline the gradual change of your hero and store this information as a General Note in Final Draft by following these steps:

1. If the Navigator window is not visible, click the **Tools** menu and choose **Show Navigator** (Macintosh) or click the **Tools** tab and click the **Show Navigator** icon.
2. Click the **ScriptNotes** tab at the top of the Navigator window. Final Draft displays all your notes.
3. Click on the Hero General Note and click in the **Note Text** box where you typed the hero's name.
4. Type a paragraph describing your hero as the complete opposite of your theme.
5. Type a second paragraph describing how the hero learns the theme from a Mentor.
6. Type a third paragraph describing a moment when the hero suddenly realizes that his old way of life (the opposite of the theme) represents a dead end.
7. Type a fourth paragraph explaining how the hero can visually show that he understands the theme that helps defeat the villain.

Exercise #12: The Hero's Goal

At the simplest level, characters need to pursue a physical goal. A physical goal is something we can see. However, what makes a physical goal more engaging is when a character has an emotional reason to achieve that physical goal. An emotional goal consists of two parts:

- A selfish reason
- A selfless reason

So every hero actually has three interrelated goals:

- A physical goal
- A selfish emotional goal
- A selfless emotional goal to save a loved one

In "Ghostbusters," the physical goal is to kill the giant marshmallow man. The selfish emotional reason is to avoid getting killed himself. The selfless emotional reason is to save his girlfriend.

In "Hugo," the physical goal is to get an automaton working. The selfish emotional goal is to satisfy his own curiosity on making the automaton work. The selfless emotional goal is to help save a bitter old man who was once a prominent film maker.

In "The Hunger Games," the physical goal is to protect her little sister. The selfish emotional goal is to survive and not get killed. The selfless emotional goal is to save Peeta, the boy who is in love with her.

Look at any bad movie and you'll often see that the story lacks a selfless emotional element. In bad martial arts movies, the hero seeks to kill someone (a physical goal) while trying to avoid getting killed (a selfish emotional goal). However, the hero has no selfless emotional reason to achieve his physical goal. The whole purpose of the movie is simply to show two people punching and kicking at each other as often as possible.

Yet take the same martial arts idea, add in a selfless emotional goal, and you get "The Karate Kid." In both the original and the remake, the hero has a physical goal (to win the love of a girl), a selfish emotional goal (to avoid getting beat up), and a selfless emotional goal (to help his martial arts teacher). By achieving the selfless emotional goal, achieving the physical goal makes the hero's triumph that much more satisfying.

Notice that when you add multiple layers of motivation, your hero's goal suddenly develops depth and becomes far more interesting than just the standard "kill the bad guy" goal of bad movies. To deepen your hero's motivation, define the following:

- The physical goal the hero needs to achieve
- The selfish reason the hero wants to achieve this goal
- The selfless reason the hero needs to save a loved one

Add this information to your hero's General Note in Final Draft by following these steps:

1. If the Navigator window is not visible, click the **Tools** menu and choose **Show Navigator** (Macintosh) or click the **Tools** tab and click the **Show Navigator** icon.
2. Click the **ScriptNotes** tab at the top of the Navigator window. Final Draft displays all your notes.
3. Click on the Hero General Note and click in the **Note Text** box where you typed the hero's name.
4. Type a paragraph describing the physical goal your hero needs to achieve to defeat the villain.
5. Type a second paragraph describing the selfish reason why the hero wants to achieve this goal.
6. Type a third paragraph describing a selfless reason the hero needs to achieve this goal to save a loved one, and identify who this loved one is.

If you look at your General Note for your hero, you should start seeing how you can view your hero's story in multiple ways from just the physical act of achieving a goal to the underlying emotional reason for pursing and achieving a goal.

By making your hero's goal more intricate and emotionally

meaningful, you increase your chances of writing a far more emotionally powerful story than just a simple "the good guy blows up the bad guy" ending that may look visually interesting, but remains emotionally empty.

Summary

In this chapter, you learned how to focus on your story as either villain-driven or hero-driven so you know how to develop your story. Then you learned how to outline your hero's gradual change based on your theme.

Finally, you learned to understand the multiple reasons why your hero needs to achieve a goal to make the achievement of that goal more emotionally satisfying. To store all this information, you've gotten more practice opening, viewing, and editing General Notes stored in your Final Draft document.

Save your document by pressing Command+S (Macintosh) or Ctrl+S (Windows). In the next chapter, you'll start defining the other characters in your story.

6 THE MENTOR, THE ALLIES, AND THE HENCHMEN

Your hero needs to defeat a villain, but she can't do it alone. More importantly, she can't do it without changing. To change, your hero needs to learn your story's theme and to do that, you hero needs to meet a Mentor.

After the hero and the villain, the Mentor is the third most important character in your story. Like the hero, the Mentor begins in a dead end life that's a direct result of a past mistake. To overcome this past mistake and escape his dead end life, the Mentor has a goal but needs the hero's help.

Initially, the hero may be reluctant to follow the Mentor, but then the villain forces the hero to act so the hero has no choice but to follow the Mentor.

In "The Karate Kid," the Mentor knows who the hero is but makes little effort to interfere in the hero's life. Only when the villain starts beating the hero up does the Mentor intervene and save the hero. The villain's actions always drive the hero to a Mentor.

In "Django Unchained," the hero is trapped in slavery when the Mentor rescues him because the hero knows the location of some wanted men. The hero has no choice but to follow the Mentor, but finds himself trapped in a saloon when the Mentor shoots the town's sheriff. Only later does he realize that the Mentor is a bounty hunter and if the hero leads the Mentor to the wanted men, the hero can get revenge on those men.

In "Avatar," the hero is exploring an alien world when he gets separated from his group and risks dying until his Mentor shows up and saves him.

The Mentor and the hero need each other. The hero needs to learn the theme, which the Mentor teaches through a visually interesting but initially confusing lesson. In return, the Mentor needs the hero's help in fixing the problems of the Mentor's past. Typically the only way the Mentor can overcome the problems of the past is by contact with the villain.

Eventually, the Mentor can no longer help the hero, which forces the hero to face the villain alone. Sometimes this means the Mentor dies (Obi-wan in "Star Wars," the butler in "Arthur," and the bounty hunter in "Django Unchained") but sometimes the Mentor lives. In either case, the hero is on his own.

The basic story line of the Mentor goes like this:

- Like the hero, the Mentor starts out stuck in a dead end life due to a past mistake
- The Mentor helps the hero and teaches the story theme as a lesson to the hero
- The Mentor is forced to abandon the hero
- The Mentor resolves the past mistake indirectly through the villain

Exercise #13: The Mentor's Story

The Mentor serves two purposes. First, the Mentor teaches the hero your story theme, often in a visually interesting manner. Second, the Mentor's pursuit of a goal often mirrors the hero's own goal, which reinforces the theme.

In "Django Unchained," the hero wants to rescue his wife from a cruel slave owner while the Mentor wants to hunt down and kill criminals.

In "The King's Speech," the hero wants to be seen as a strong leader who can speak clearly while the Mentor wants to prove that his unorthodox teaching methods work.

In "The Sixth Sense," the hero wants to help a boy deal with his problem while the Mentor (the little boy) wants to find a way to deal with his problem of seeing dead people.

By knowing how your Mentor changes and resolves a problem from the past, you can create a secondary story that supports your main story in a way that seems natural and not forced. When a Mentor teaches a hero but doesn't have a goal of his own, the Mentor's appearance feels contrived. When the Mentor pursues a goal similar to the hero's goal, then the Mentor's appearance strengthens your overall story.

Let's store the four elements of your Mentor's story in the General Note describing your Mentor's name by following these steps:

1. If the Navigator window is not visible, click the **Tools** menu and choose **Show Navigator** (Macintosh) or click the **Tools** tab and click the **Show Navigator** icon.
2. Click the **ScriptNotes** tab at the top of the Navigator window. Final Draft displays all your notes.
3. Click on the Mentor General Note and click in the **Note Text** box where you typed the mentor's name.
4. Type a paragraph describing the past mistake that your Mentor wants to resolve.
5. Type a second paragraph describing how your Mentor teaches your hero the theme in a visually interesting way.
6. Type a third paragraph describing how and why your Mentor abandons the hero.
7. Type a fourth paragraph explaining how the Mentor resolves his past mistake through contact with the villain.

Notice that great movies have a Mentor pursuing a clear goal involving the villain that gets resolved somehow. Think of "Star Wars," "The Karate Kid," "The King's Speech," and "Up," which all have both strong heroes and Mentor characters that teach the hero how to become a better person.

Bad movies only focus on the hero. Good movies focus on the hero and mirror the hero's story in all the other characters. You want to write a good movie, so flesh out the details of your Mentor.

Exercise #14: The Allies

Your story is about your hero, but your hero can never defeat the more powerful villain all by herself. To have a chance, your hero needs help.

The Mentor teaches your hero the story theme that helps change her into a better person with the capability of defeating the villain. However, your hero still can't fight the villain alone. To do that, the hero needs the help of one or more allies.

Like the hero, allies are also in pursuit of a goal. In many cases, allies have the same type of goal as the hero. In "Legally Blonde," the hero wants to find love. She befriends a hairdresser who also wants to find love in the arms of a handsome UPS deliveryman. The hairdresser helps the hero and the hero turns around and teaches her ally how to get the attention of the UPS deliveryman.

Where the Mentor teaches the hero, the hero teaches the allies.

The allies change over time just like the hero:

- When the hero first meets the allies, they're stuck in a dead end life, searching for a goal
- The allies help the hero deal with being in an unfamiliar world
- The hero teaches the allies how to achieve their goal
- The allies achieve their goal

In "Star Wars," Luke meets his ally, Hans Solo, who looks out only for himself. Luke needs Hans to pilot a starship to get him off his planet. When the Death Star captures them, Luke wants to rescue Princess Leia, which shows Hans that money doesn't always have to be the motivation.

Just when Luke is about to get shot down by Darth Vader, Hans appears out of nowhere and shoots down Darth Vader's escorts, knocking Darth Vader off course so Luke can get a clear shot at the Death Star. By saving Luke, Hans has changed for the better.

Allies always change and gain a better life directly through the hero's influence.

In "WALL-E," WALL-E gains several allies. First are a couple looking for love, just like WALL-E. Second is the starship captain who's bored out of his mind. Third are a group of defective robots that don't want to be reprogrammed.

WALL-E helps bring the couple together so they can meet and fall in love. Then WALL-E's actions encourage the starship captain to stand up to the villain and take back control of the starship. Finally, WALL-E's actions help the defective robots rebel against the villain. By the end of the story, every ally is in a happier situation than before.

The four elements of a change for each ally include:

- An ally is stuck in a dead end life
- The allies help the hero
- The hero turns around and helps the allies
- Based on the hero's help, the allies get a better life for themselves

Right now, you've only created a General Note for one ally. Your story will need at least one ally, but most likely you'll have two or more allies. That means you'll need to create one or more additional General Notes and name them something like Ally #1, Ally #2, and so on.

How many allies do you need? As few as possible. Think of each ally as someone who your hero absolutely needs.

In "Star Wars,"" Luke can't get off his planet by himself, so he absolutely needs someone who can pilot a starship. That's Hans. Later, Luke absolutely needs to join the rebels, and he can't do that without the help of Princess Leia. That's why Luke has two allies.

In "The Hunger Games," Katniss needs Peeta to make her look more appealing by proclaiming his love for her on national TV. Second, Katniss needs the help of a little girl, Rue, who helps her escape from being trapped in a tree.

In "The Artist," the hero needs his dog to call the police and save his life when he nearly dies in a burning home. The hero also needs his loyal chauffeur to care for him when he's alone.

Your ally serves two purposes. One, the ally can move the story along when the hero cannot. In "Aliens," someone needs to crawl through a pipe to reach a station to signal for a second drop ship to come and pick them up. The hero can't do that because it would take her out of the rest of the story.

Two, an ally has skills or abilities that the hero needs. In "Aliens," the hero doesn't have the ability or knowledge to fight an army of aliens, but her allies, the Marine soldiers, do have that capability.

From an audience's point of view, allies have their own goals. From a writer's point of view, allies exist solely to help the hero. The goals of the allies must mirror the goals of the hero to support the main story.

Since your allies only exist to help the hero (although you have to give them their own goals to disguise this fact), the number and types of allies your story needs depends entirely on your hero's pursuit of a goal. The more details you know about your hero's pursuit of a goal, the better you'll know when your hero hits a dead end and needs an ally.

At this point, you may only have a rough idea about the details of your hero's story, so define at least one ally. When you know more about your plot details, then you may discover you need another ally with unique skills that can help the hero in ways that the hero can't do herself.

It's time to create the four elements of one ally's story in the General Note describing your ally's name by following these steps:

1. If the Navigator window is not visible, click the **Tools** menu and choose **Show Navigator** (Macintosh) or click the **Tools** tab and click the **Show Navigator** icon.
2. Click the **ScriptNotes** tab at the top of the Navigator window. Final Draft displays all your notes.
3. Click on the Allies General Note and click in the **Note Text** box where you typed the ally's name.
4. Type a paragraph describing how the ally is stuck in a dead end life with a goal similar to the hero's dead end life and goal.
5. Type a second paragraph describing how the skill of the ally can help the hero in a way that the hero can't do herself.
6. Type a third paragraph describing how the hero helps the ally achieve his goal.
7. Type a fourth paragraph describing how the ally winds up in a better life.

Remember, your story needs at least one ally and will likely have two or more allies. When you define the plot, you'll know what others allies your hero may need to achieve her ultimate goal.

Exercise #15: The Henchmen

There's rarely a single villain opposing the hero. In a villain-driven story, the main villain can't fight the hero too soon or the entire story would be over. Instead, the main villain sends his henchmen to attack the hero.

In a hero-driven story, there is no single dominant villain, so you wind up with multiple villains popping up just enough to cause problems for the hero. In both cases, you always have multiple villains attacking your hero.

On the simplest level, one or more henchmen just keep attacking the hero over and over again until the hero finally defeats them, much like James Bond endlessly battling people trying to kill him. Yet such endless (and mindless) battles can get tiresome after a while. (Just watch any bad James Bond movie to see this endless battle between James Bond and the villain's henchmen over and over again.)

A better solution is to give your henchmen a goal of their own. This not only makes the henchmen seem interesting, but also makes the battle between the hero and the henchmen more emotionally satisfying. Ideally, the goals of the henchmen should also clash with the main villain's goals, to give both the villain and the henchmen conflict with each other.

In "Die Hard," the main villain orders his henchmen to hunt down and kill the hero. However, the hero has killed the brother of one of the henchmen, so now the surviving brother is highly motivated to kill the hero. Yet his zeal for killing the hero also endangers the villain's main goal at times, which creates conflict and provides a richer, more complex understanding of the villain beyond just having a bad guy (and his henchmen) doing bad things for no reason.

Your story's henchmen are like the opposite of your story's allies. Where the allies exist only when the hero needs help, henchmen exist solely to make the hero's life as difficult as possible. Henchmen must always be more powerful than the hero with the sole goal of stopping the hero from achieving her goal.

Ideally, each henchmen tries a different way to stop the hero. This creates variety while also forcing the hero to keep changing.

In "Finding Nemo," one of the first henchman to stop the hero is a shark. A second henchman is similar to the shark, but is a blind, carnivorous fish that just wants to eat the hero like the shark wanted to.

However, a third henchman is a school of jellyfish, which forces the hero to realize he needs his Mentor, Dory the forgetful fish. When Dory gets stung, the hero has to save her.

A fourth henchman is the whale, which teaches the hero that sometimes you have to just let go and take your chances. A fifth henchman are the flock of pigeons trying to eat him. The sixth henchman are the fishermen, who give the hero a chance to let go and trust his son's judgement.

Henchmen don't exist just to make life difficult for the hero, but to force the hero to learn something from the Mentor. The Mentor teaches the hero a lesson, but the henchmen force the hero to understand that lesson.

So henchmen provide two purposes. First, they allow the villain to attack the hero since the main villain must wait until the end to attack the hero. Second, henchmen force the hero to change based on the Mentor's lesson.

With every henchman, make sure you clarify the henchman's motive for attacking the hero. Without a clear motive for the henchman, the henchman's battle with the hero will seem contrived and phony.

You'll likely have more than one henchman, but for each one, define the following:

- What motive does your henchman have for attacking the hero? The clearer this motive, the more threatening the henchman will be.
- What special skill does the henchman have to threaten the

hero? This skill makes the henchman more powerful than the hero.

- How can the henchman force the hero to learn the Mentor's lesson (your story theme)?
- How does the hero defeat the henchman?

Since you know you'll have at least one henchman, store this information as a General Note in Final Draft by following these steps:

1. If the Navigator window is not visible, click the **Tools** menu and choose **Show Navigator** (Macintosh) or click the **Tools** tab and click the **Show Navigator** icon.
2. Click the **ScriptNotes** tab at the top of the Navigator window. Final Draft displays all your notes.
3. Click on the Henchman General Note and click in the **Note Text** box where you typed the henchman's name.
4. Type a paragraph describing your henchman's motive.
5. Type a second paragraph describing a visually interesting skill that your henchman can use to show he's more powerful than the hero.
6. Type a third paragraph describing how the henchman can force the hero to learn the story theme (not always possible with every henchman).
7. Type a fourth paragraph explaining how the hero defeats the henchman.

Like allies, keep the number of henchmen down to a bare minimum. The fewer characters you have, the more you can focus on each of them to make your story feel stronger as a result.

Summary

In this chapter, you learned how to flesh out details about your three major secondary characters, the Mentor, an ally, and a henchmen. You'll likely have two or more allies and henchmen, but you'll only have a single Mentor.

Mentors are more complex than allies and henchmen. Allies exist only when your hero absolutely cannot do anything more on her own. Henchmen exist to harass the hero, force the hero to learn the story's theme, and save the most powerful villain for the final climactic battle at the end.

Allies need goals of their own to make them feel like real people and to mirror the theme and hero's goal. Henchmen also need goals of their own, although their goals are often much simpler than the goals of the hero's allies.

Save your document by pressing Command+S (Macintosh) or Ctrl+S (Windows). In the next chapter, you'll start structuring your story.

7 THE FOUR ACTS OF A SCREENPLAY

A typical screenplay is 120 pages long where each page represents one minute. Comedy and horror movies are often shorter at 90 pages, but some movies go much longer. The longer the movie, the less times a theater can show it and the more expensive it will be to produce. For that reason, most screenplays range between 90 - 120 pages in length.

Whatever the length of the screenplay, screenwriters typically divide a story into three Acts:

- Act I - 30 minutes
- Act II - 60 minutes
- Act III - 30 minutes

The biggest problem with seeing your story as three Acts is that Act II is twice as long as the other two Acts. It actually makes more sense to divide a story into four Acts:

- Act I - 30 minutes (Exposition)
- Act IIa - 30 minutes (Positive rising action)
- Act IIb - 30 minutes (Negative rising action)
- Act III - 30 minutes (Climax)

Act I introduces the main characters and the story. This is where we learn what's going on, who the hero is, what the hero wants, and the obstacles stopping the hero.

Act IIa shows the hero pursuing an initial goal, making allies, and generally succeeding in moving closer to a goal

Act IIb shows the hero facing major setbacks as the villain seems overpowering to the point of nearly killing the hero's dream of achieving the final goal altogether.

Act III shows the final battle to the death between the hero and the villain. The hero and villain have mutually exclusive goals so if the hero wins, the villain must lose. If the villain wins, the hero must lose. This forces both the hero and the villain to fight to the bitter end to get what they want.

When you divide a screenplay into four Acts, you can better understand the story structure of a screenplay. This is how the four Act story structure looks in "Django Unchained":

- Act I - The hero is trapped as a slave, but gets rescued by a Mentor who turns out to be a bounty hunter. The hero's goal from the start is to rescue his wife from slavery.
- Act IIa - The hero helps the Mentor track down some criminals. In return, the Mentor teaches the hero how to shoot and decides to help him find his wife. So far, life looks like it's getting better for the hero.
- Act IIb - The hero finds the plantation where his wife is being held and he and the Mentor create a plan to rescue her, but the villain discovers the plan. The Mentor dies, leaving the hero alone as a slave again.
- Act III - Using the skills he learned from the Mentor, the hero escapes and goes back to free his wife.

Act I must grab our attention, reveal a sympathetic hero, and define the goal the hero pursues so we know where the story is go.

Act IIa throws the hero into a new world where the hero may face minor setbacks, but gains allies. The hero often learns the Mentor's lesson (the story's theme) and becomes more powerful than before.

Act IIb is where everything starts falling apart for the hero. The villain often makes the hero's life much harder and nearly destroys the hero altogether, but the hero barely survives and realizes that he can't win unless he changes somehow.

Act III is really what your story is all about. This is where the rebels fight Darth Vader for control of the galaxy ("Star Wars"), where your hero confronts the villain face to face to a final battle where only one will survive ("Kill Bill"), where the initial goal defined in the beginning is finally within reach ("The Terminator").

The four Act structure defines the flow of every story. First, the hero starts off wanting a goal (Act I). Second, the hero makes progress towards achieving that goal (Act IIa). Third, the hero faces setbacks blocking that goal (Act IIb). Finally, the hero risks everything to achieve the initial goal that started the story from the beginning (Act III).

Exercise #16: Structuring the Four Acts of Your Screenplay with the Hero

To structure your screenplay, you need to focus on what belongs in each Act. That means creating four new General Notes where each General Note describes what happens in one entire Act.

Don't worry about being "right" at this point or not. The main goal is to toss in ideas that you think should go in each Act. Later you can delete, edit, or move ideas from one Act to another if you wish.

Let's start by creating four new General Notes by following these steps:

1. Click on the Hero General Note. From Exercises #10b and 11, you should have four paragraphs that define what happens in each Act. Select and copy the text that belongs

in Act I.

2. Click the **Insert** menu and choose **General Note** (Macintosh) or click the **Insert** tab and click the **General Note** icon. Final Draft creates a blank General Note in the Navigator window.

3. Click in the **Name** text box and type **Act I**.

4. Click in the **Color** popup menu and choose a color such as Purple.

5. Click in the **Type** popup menu and choose **New Type.** A New ScriptNotes Type dialog box appears.

6. Type **Act I** (or any descriptive phrase you want to associate with Act I) and click **OK**.

7. Click in the **Note Text** box and paste the text you copied in step 1 from your Hero General Note.

8. Repeat steps 1-7 except in step 3 and 6, create a General Note for Act IIa, IIb, and III.

In Exercises #10b and #11, you outlined the basic four-part structure of how your hero begins with an initial goal (Act I), how your hero starts to change (Act IIa), how your hero hits a major obstacle (Act IIb), and how your hero finally achieves that initial goal. By focusing on the changes each of your major characters go through, you can clearly see what type of information you need to introduce in each Act.

Bad movies fail for multiple reasons. One, bad movies often introduce something in one Act but fail to use that information anywhere else. Two, bad movies may introduce something in a later Act that was never introduced earlier, so it seems to come out of nowhere and have no relevance to the rest of the story.

Three, bad movies don't develop characters to show how they change over time. Instead, characters remain static or even worse, change in ways that don't support the story's theme. This results in a disjointed story. Instead of telling a single story, a bad movie tries to tell multiple stories that don't seem related in any way. The end result is a bunch of half-developed ideas that makes the movie feel incomplete and unsatisfying.

To avoid this problem, first outline the basic changes of all your major characters and then organize them in separate Acts. Now you'll not only know what type of information goes into each Act, but you'll also know what you need to create a complete story.

Exercise #17: Structuring the Four Acts of Your Screenplay with the Villain

After your hero, your villain is the second most important character in your story. Without a villain, your hero has nobody to fight against. With no fight, there's no conflict and with no conflict, there's no story.

Even if you create a hero-driven story without a single, dominant villain, you need a villain (along with one or more henchmen) to harass the hero. The villain serves two purposes. One, the villain's conflict with the hero forces the hero to change and take action. Two, the villain must be defeated to make the story feel complete and satisfying.

In "The Hunger Games," the main villain is the President, who oppresses the other Districts with the Hunger Games where kids must fight to the death. His henchmen include the game maker and the other contestants who threaten the hero.

"The Hunger Games" feels complete because the other contestants die, the game maker is forced to commit suicide, and the President winds up feeling like a loser as the hero has defied his authority by winning and rallying the other districts as a symbol of resistance. In "The Hunger Games," every villain loses, and that makes the story feel complete and satisfying.

Now look at the sequel, "Catching Fire." Once again, the villain is the President and the henchmen include the other game contestants but also a cruel commander who takes over District 12, the hero's home district.

At the end of "Catching Fire," the hero escapes, foiling the President, the other game contestants are killed, but the cruel commander is nowhere to be seen. He's evil, he threatens the hero, but in the end, he escapes unscathed. This incompleteness makes "Catching Fire" far less emotionally satisfying than "The Hunger Games."

Think of any good movie and the villain (and his henchmen) all get defeated. Every good James Bond movie ends in complete defeat of the villain. Now imagine if James Bond failed to defeat the villain. That would make the story feel incomplete. James Bond doesn't always kill every henchmen, but he neutralizes them so they're no longer a threat to himself any more.

Think of how satisfying "Jaws" would have been if the hero never killed the shark? How satisfying would "The Terminator" have been if we never saw the hero crush the Terminator to death? Every villain in your story must be defeated.

Even in hero-driven stories where villains aren't necessarily working together, you need to structure how your villains interact with your hero. In "Finding Nemo," the hero escapes from a shark, a blind fish, jellyfish, a whale, a flock of pigeons, and some fishermen. The hero doesn't need to wipe out the villains, but he does need to neutralize them so they're no longer a threat. If your hero doesn't defeat every villain (and henchman) in your story, your story isn't finished yet.

In "Die Hard," the hero has wiped out all the henchmen and even the villain. At the end, the final henchmen shows up with a machine gun, ready to gun down the hero. That's when the hero's Mentor (the black police officer who feared he could no longer draw his gun), pulls out his gun and shoots the final henchman.

Every time the villain and a henchman get defeated, that makes the story emotionally satisfying. When all the henchmen and the villain get defeated, that makes the story complete.

If you're creating a villain-driven story, let's take your basic ideas and put them in the right Acts of your screenplay. If you're creating a hero-driven story, you probably didn't do Exercise #10a so skip to Exercise #18.

1. Click on the Villain General Note. If you did Exercise #10a, you you should have four paragraphs that define what happens in each Act. Select and copy the text that belongs in Act I.
2. Click the **Insert** menu and choose **General Note** (Macintosh) or click the **Insert** tab and click the **General Note** icon. Final Draft creates a blank General Note in the Navigator window.
3. Click in the **Name** text box and type **Act I.**
4. Click in the **Color** popup menu and choose a color such as Purple.
5. Click in the **Type** popup menu and choose **New Type.** A New ScriptNotes Type dialog box appears.
6. Type **Act I** (or any descriptive phrase you want to associate with Act I) and click **OK.**
7. Click in the **Note Text** box and paste the text you copied in step 1 from your Hero General Note.
8. Repeat steps 1-7 except in step 3 and 6, create a General Note for Act IIa, IIb, and III.

Exercise #18: Adding the Villain's Influence on the Four Acts of Your Screenplay

In both a villain-driven and a hero-driven story, the villain (or villains) gets progressively more dangerous. In "Finding Nemo," the shark is dangerous, but he's held back by his other shark buddies. The blind, carnivorous fish is slightly more dangerous because there's nothing holding him back from trying to eat the hero.

The jellyfish are dangerous in a different way because they aren't actively trying to kill the hero. Instead, they threaten the hero by threatening the hero's Mentor. For the first time, the hero has to worry about saving someone other than himself. Any time you have to save others, the task is more difficult.

The whale is the next henchmen that isn't even trying to kill the hero or the Mentor, but the whale's huge size poses a different and bigger problem. Each threat to the hero must be different to avoid repetition.

After the hero escapes from the whale, the next villain are the pigeons who want to eat him. When the hero escapes from this threat, the final villain are the fishermen.

In a villain-driven story, you also have this steady progression of more difficult and more challenging henchmen threatening the hero. In both cases, the villain and henchmen are always forcing the hero to change into a better person.

Remember, the real purpose of the villain isn't just to fight the hero or else you get an endless amount of pointless action like a bad martial arts movie. The villain really forces the hero to change.

In "Star Wars," Luke would never have agreed to leave with Obi-wan if Darth Vader's stormtroopers hadn't wiped out his uncle and aunt. Luke would never have found the courage to rescue Princess Leia if Darth Vader hadn't captured her. Luke never would have blown up the Death Star if Darth Vader wasn't trying to wipe out the rebel base with it. You can think of your villain as a demented and twisted teacher to your hero.

While the Mentor gently teaches the hero a lesson (your story's theme), your villain harshly teaches that same lesson through negative examples. Your villain is actually a cruel teacher that makes your hero learn your story's theme.

The basic four-part structure of the villain's story looks like this:

- The villain defines the hero's goal
- The villain demonstrates Horrible Consequences should the hero fail
- The villain nearly defeats the hero
- The villain forces a final showdown with the hero

In a villain-driven story like "Star Wars," the villain creates the final obstacle for the hero. In a hero-driven story like "Little Miss Sunshine," the villain blocks the hero from achieving the initial goal.

In "Star Wars," the villain blows up a planet to demonstrate the fate that could occur at the end if the hero fails. In "Little Miss Sunshine," the first villain (the van breaking down) threatens to keep the hero from attending the beauty pageant.

In "Star Wars," the villain nearly corners the hero. In "Little Miss Sunshine," the villain (a police officer) threatens to stop the hero and arrest the father for illegally transporting a dead body across state lines.

In "Star Wars," the villain plans to destroy the rebel base but the hero wants to save the rebel base. In "Little Miss Sunshine," the villain tries to yank the hero off the stage but the hero and her family defend and support her.

In both villain-driven and hero-driven stories, each Act of your screenplay makes life harder as the villain constantly threatens the hero. Now flesh out the structure of your four General Notes for Act I, Act IIa, Act IIb, and Act III to inject the villain's influence on your story:

1. Click on the Act I General Note.
2. Click in the **Note Text** box and write a paragraph that describes how your villain represents the obstacle to your hero's final goal.
3. Click on the Act IIa General Note and add a second paragraph describing what the villain can do to demonstrate the threat that the hero will face in the final climactic showdown.
4. Click on the Act IIa General Note and add a third paragraph describing how the villain nearly defeats the hero.
5. Click on the Act III General Note and add a fourth paragraph describing the final showdown between the hero

and the villain.

At this point, you should have a basic outline of how your story will work. In each Act, you have ideas for what needs to occur with both your hero and your villain. Now it's time to finish filling out each Act with the secondary characters, the Mentor, the allies, and the henchmen.

Exercise #19: The Mentor, Allies, and Henchmen

Like the hero and villain, the secondary characters often appear in every Act of your story, although their role is always much smaller. In some stories, the hero doesn't meet any allies until Act IIa.

Once you've organized how your hero and villain gradually change over each Act, you need to define how your Mentor, allies, and henchmen also appear and change over each Act. Doing this keeps your story from dragging by only focusing on the hero or villain, which gives your story greater depth. Switching the focus from the hero or villain to the Mentor, allies, and henchmen often provides a break in the main story and shows how subplots involving these secondary characters directly affects the hero and villain.

Since you've already written down notes about your Mentor, allies, and henchmen, you just need to copy an paste this information into the different Act I, Act IIa, Act IIb, and Act III General Notes in Final Draft by following these steps:

1. Click on the Mentor General Note and click in the **Note Text** box where you typed the Mentor's name. From Exercise #13, you should have four paragraphs that define the four changes that your Mentor goes through. Select and copy the first paragraph that belongs in Act I.
2. Click on the Act I General Note and paste the text.
3. Repeat steps 1 and 2 except for the text that belongs in Act IIa, Act IIb, and Act III.
4. Click on the Allies General Note and click in the **Note Text**

box where you typed the Ally's name. From Exercise #14, you should have four paragraphs that define the four changes that your ally goes through. Select and copy the first paragraph that belongs in Act I. (Note: Allies often don't appear until Act IIa, so you might not need to paste any information in the Act I General Note.)

5. Click on the Act I General Note and paste the text.
6. Repeat steps 4 and 5 except for the text that belongs in Act IIa, Act IIb, and Act III.
7. Click on the Henchmen General Note and click in the **Note Text** box where you typed the Henchman's name. From Exercise #15, you should have four paragraphs that define the four changes that your henchman goes through. Select and copy the first paragraph that belongs in Act I.
8. Click on the Act I General Note and paste the text.
9. Repeat steps 7 and 8 except for the text that belongs in Act IIa, Act IIb, and Act III.

At this point, your Act I, Act IIa, Act IIb, and Act III General Notes should have information about all of your major characters. Now you can insure that each Act of your story tells every major character's story so your overall story and each character's change feels complete.

Summary

In this chapter, you learned how to divide a screenplay into four Acts where each Act typically represents 30 minutes out of a 120-minute screenplay. By taking your notes that you created earlier, describing the gradual change for your major characters, you can see where each character's information needs to be placed in your story.

In Act I, you should have the following:

- The initial goal your hero and villain are pursuing.
- The hero's dead end life that represents the opposite of your story's theme.

- The Mentor's dead end life due to a past mistake.
- How your hero meets the Mentor.
- The henchman's motive for wanting to attack the hero.
- The ally's dead end life (In some stories, the ally doesn't appear until Act IIa)

In Act IIa, you should have the following:

- How your villain inadvertently interferes in your hero's life, forcing your hero to act.
- How your Mentor teaches the hero a lesson based on your story's theme.
- The first stepping stone the hero takes towards achieving an initial goal.
- How your hero meets one or more allies.
- The ally's dead end life (if this isn't already defined in Act I).
- The special skills or power that the henchmen have to defeat the hero.

In Act IIb, you should have the following:

- How your villain tries to wipe out the hero.
- A second major stepping stone your hero gets towards the initial goal.
- How your hero suddenly realizes that his or her old way of life is a dead end.
- How the Mentor must abandon the hero.
- How the hero helps an ally learn to reach his or her goal.
- How the henchman can force the hero to realize his or her life is a dead end.

In Act III, you should have the following:

- How the villain is on the verge of success.
- The internal conflict the hero must overcome.
- How the hero embraces the Mentor's lesson (your story

theme).

- How the Mentor resolves the mistakes from the past.
- How the ally achieves his or her initial goal.
- How the hero defeats the henchman.
- How the hero defeats the villain by using the Mentor's lesson.

Notice how a fully developed story consists of multiple story lines, yet if you tried to focus on your hero, you'll risk omitting crucial details of your other characters. By first plotting out the changes of your major characters and then arranging them in different Acts, you can better see how your overall story flows. Best of all, you created a rough outline of your story without writing a single word of your script.

Most people make the mistake of writing their screenplay without knowing what their story is all about. Given the limited amount of space available in a screenplay, it's far easier to plot the rough outline of your story ahead of time and then write a screenplay once you know how your story progresses. It's much easier to edit a few lines of text than multiple pages of a 120-page screenplay.

Save your document by pressing Command+S (Macintosh) or Ctrl+S (Windows). In the next chapter, you'll start actually using Final Draft to turn your story idea into a screenplay.

Wallace Wang

8 CREATING AND MANIPULATING SCENES

Think of your favorite movie and chances are good you'll remember a handful of notable scenes. Think about the original "The Karate Kid" and you probably remember the famous wax on, wax off scene along with the crane stance at the end. Think about "Raiders of the Lost Ark" and you likely remember the giant boulder rolling towards Indiana Jones, Indiana Jones pulling out his pistol to shoot a sword wielding attacker, and the Nazis opening up the ark only to have ghostly spirits decimate them all. Think about "Jaws" and you remember a giant shark's mouth rising out of the ocean.

Every good movie has a handful of iconic, memorable scenes. Chances are good that when you came up with your story idea, you already visualized a handful of memorable scenes for your own screenplay. Even if you don't use these memorable scenes, it's important to write them down because they're part of your original inspiration for your story idea.

In an actual script, you identify the beginning of every scene with the following elements:

- Scene description either inside (INT.) or outside (EXT.)
- Scene location such as RESTAURANT or BAR
- Scene time such as DAY or NIGHT, but if necessary for

your scene, you can also define a more specific time period such as EARLY MORNING or DUSK

Some examples of scene headings look like this:

EXT. B-2 BOMBER - NIGHT

INT. BULLET TRAIN- DAY

EXT. FRONT YARD - DUSK

INT. HOUSE - MORNING

The scene heading (also called a slug line) provides just enough information that's absolutely crucial, but nothing more. If your scene must take place in the early morning, then it's okay to specify EARLY MORNING. If your scene only needs to take place during the day, then just specify DAY.

The ultimate goal of writing, and screenwriting in particular, is to paint a visual image in the reader's mind using as few words as possible. If your scene can take place inside any car, then just mention CAR. If your scene absolutely must take place inside a specific car, such as a Lamborghini, then it's okay to specify INT. LAMBORGHINI - DAY.

Each time you specify a new scene heading, the action physically takes place in another location. So you may see a scene heading that defines action taking place inside a bar, then another scene heading later in the script defining the action taking place outside on the street.

Scene headings always need to be capitalized. Since turning Caps Lock on and off all the time can be cumbersome, Final Draft can automatically format text based on different styles. To format scene headings properly, Final Draft offers a (you guessed it) Scene Heading style. When you choose the Scene Heading style, Final Draft automatically capitalizes everything you type and correctly formats your text.

Final Draft's automatic formatting capabilities are the prime reason screenwriters use Final Draft instead of ordinary word processors to write screenplays. That way they can focus on writing and let Final Draft worry about the formatting details.

Exercise #20: Creating Scene Headings

With your knowledge of scene headings and your ideas of memorable scenes in your screenplay, it's time to capture these ideas down and actually use Final Draft's automatic screenplay formatting features.

When you create a new Final Draft document or open an existing document, Final Draft displays a big window on the left where you can type your actual screenplay. Let's see how to create scene headings in Final Draft. Make sure your Final Draft document is open and follow these steps:

1. Click in the document window.
2. Press **ENTER** on the keyboard. An Elements window pops up, listing all the format styles Final Draft offers as shown in Figure 8-1.

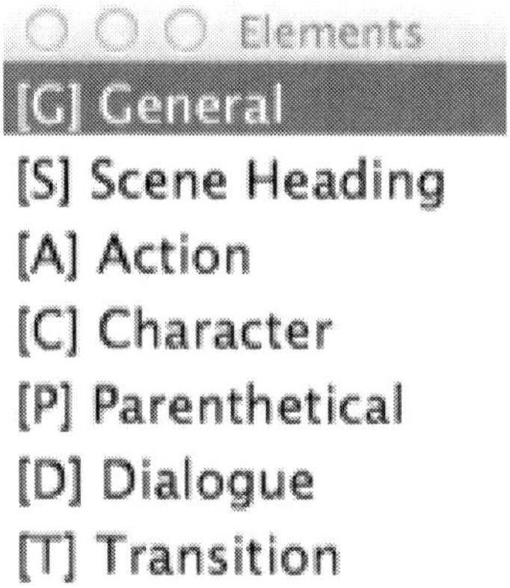

○ ○ ○ Elements

[G] General

[S] Scene Heading

[A] Action

[C] Character

[P] Parenthetical

[D] Dialogue

[T] Transition

Figure 8-1. The Elements window lets you choose a formatting style.

3. Type **S** or use the arrow keys to highlight [S] Scene

Heading and press **ENTER**. Final Draft displays the current format style at the bottom of the document window as shown in Figure 8-2. (Hint: With the Macintosh version of Final Draft, you can also choose the formatting style by clicking on this formatting style label so a menu pops up as shown in Figure 8-3, then choose the formatting style you want to use such as Scene Heading.)

Figure 8-2. The current formatting style appears at the bottom of the document window.

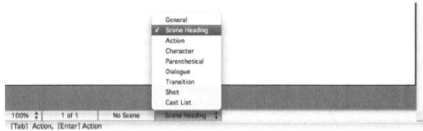

Figure 8-3. The formatting style popup menu in the Macintosh version of Final Draft.

4. Type **ext**. and press the **SPACEBAR**. Notice that as you type, Final Draft automatically capitalizes your text.
5. Type **HOUSE** (or any location), press the **SPACEBAR**, type -, and press the **SPACEBAR**.
6. Type **DA**. As you type, a SmartType window pops up as shown in Figure 8-4. The SmartType window tries to guess what you want to type so all you have to do is highlight the SmartType word suggestion and press **ENTER** to let Final Draft finish typing the text for you.

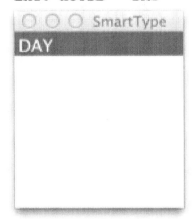

Figure 8-4. The SmartType window tries to guess what you want to type.

7. Make sure DAY is highlighted and press **ENTER**. Final Draft finishes typing the word DAY in your scene heading.
8. Type a brief description of one scene you can visualize in Act I. Feel free to browse through all the General Notes you've saved up until this point to reference your previously written ideas.
9. Repeat steps 2 - 8 to write a scene heading for Act IIa, Act IIb, and Act III. By the end, you should have four scene headings with four brief descriptions of one scene that occurs in each Act as shown in Figure 8-5.

```
EXT. HOUSE - DAY

A German officer arrives at farmhouse to interrogate a dairy
farmer. He gradually breaks down the dairy farmer's willpower
until the dairy farmer finally reveals the hidden location of
the refugees.


INT. CAFE - DAY

A German soldier flirts with a French girl and reveals that
he's a celebrity.


INT. BAR - NIGHT

A German officer discovers a British spy's ruse and a gun
battle takes place.


INT. MOVIE THEATER - NIGHT

The French girl shoots the German soldier and her helper
locks all the doors and sets the theater on fire.
```

Figure 8-5. Four scene headings in the document window.

The SmartType feature comes in handy when you start typing the same locations in your scene headings. Final Draft remembers all the scene locations you've used before so when you start typing the same location, the SmartType window will appear. By using SmartType, you can spend less time typing repetitive text so you'll have more time to think creatively about your screenplay.

Exercise #21: Displaying Scenes as Index Cards

Once you've typed several scene headings in your document, you may wonder what happens if you want to rearrange scenes. In a traditional word processor, you'd have to select and cut all the text for an entire scene, move the cursor to a new location in your screenplay, and then paste your text.

While this method can work, it's clumsy, slow, and error-prone. Fortunately, Final Draft provides a simpler solution by letting you look at each of your scenes as a series of index cards. Not only does this index card view let you see all your scenes, but it also lets you easily rearrange scenes in any order.

Final Draft provides two ways to display your scenes as index cards:

- Index Cards - Summary
- Index Cards - Script

Index Cards - Summary only displays your scene headings and nothing else. This view lets you focus solely on your scene locations as shown in Figure 8-6.

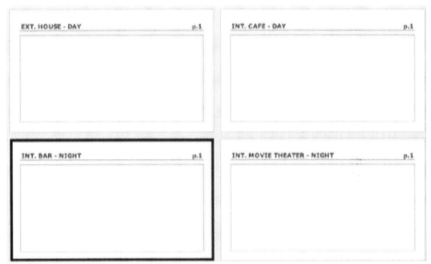

Figure 8-6. The Index Cards - Summary view only displays your scene headings.

Index Cards - Script displays your scene headings on index cards, but also displays the actual script that appears within that scene. That way you can view the descriptions, dialogue, and actions of the characters within each scene as shown in Figure 8-7.

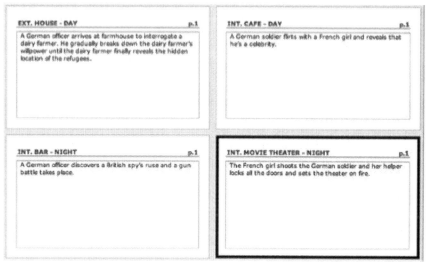

Figure 8-7. The Index Cards - Script view displays both scene headings and the actual text from each scene.

To rearrange scenes, you just drag each index card to a new location and Final Draft takes care of moving all the text in each scene automatically. Now you can focus on organizing your scenes and less on the actual mechanics of moving chunks of text around.

Let's see how to use the two different index card views to organize your screenplay. With your document open with your four scene headings typed in your document, follow these steps:

1. Click the **View** menu and choose **Index Cards - Summary** (Macintosh) or click the **View** tab and click the **Index Cards - Summary** icon. Final Draft displays your scene headings on index cards (see Figure 8-6).

2. Click the **View** menu and choose **Index Cards - Script** (Macintosh) or click the **View** tab and click the **Index Cards - Script** icon. Final Draft displays your scene headings and text of the scene on index cards (see Figure 8-7).

3. Move the mouse pointer anywhere on the bottom right index card and drag it to the upper left corner. Final Draft moves the entire index card to the front of your script. Although you can't see it yet, moving the index card

physically moves all the text of that scene in your screenplay.

4. Click the **View** menu and choose **Cards Across** (Macintosh) or click the **View** tab and click the bottom half of the **Cards Across** icon. Final Draft displays a submenu listing numbers 1 through 9.

5. Click on number **3**. Final Draft displays your index cards smaller to fit three across as shown in Figure 8-8.

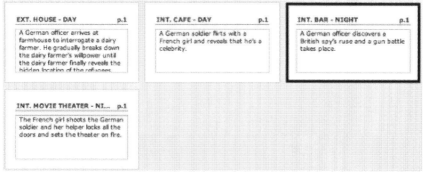

Figure 8-8. You can choose to display more or less index cards across the screen.

The more index cards you choose to display horizontally across the screen, the less you'll be able to see of each index card. However, shrinking your index cards down lets you review the overall flow of all your scenes. Then you can switch to displaying fewer index cards across if you want to study the text of each scene.

Final Draft offers another way to display your scenes called Scene View, which displays all your scenes stacked on top of each other as shown in Figure 8-9.

Figure 8-9. Scene View displays your scenes in an stack.

Besides letting you examine the flow of your scenes and rearrange them by dragging them, Scene View also lets you type a descriptive Scene Title. Any text you type in your Scene Title won't appear anywhere in your script since the Script Title is solely for you to label a particular scene for your own use.

Exercise #22: Displaying the Scene View

To view your screenplay in Scene View, follow these steps:

1. Click **View** menu and choose **Scene View** (Macintosh) or click the **View** tab and click the **Scene View** icon. Final Draft your screenplay in Scene View (see Figure 8-9).
2. Move the mouse pointer over any scene and drag the mouse to move the scene to a new location. Just like rearranging index cards, moving scenes in the Scene View physically moves that scene and all its text to a new location in your script.
3. Double-click on the **Add Scene Title** text of any scene. Final Draft displays a blank text box for you to type in.

4. Type a descriptive name for your scene and press **ENTER.** Final Draft stores your scene title in the scene.
5. Click **View** menu and choose **Script - Normal View** (Macintosh) or click the **View** tab and click the **Normal View** icon. Final Draft displays your screenplay again.

Final Draft can display your screenplay in three different views:

- Normal View — displays page breaks as horizontal lines
- Page View — displays pages so you can see top, bottom, left, and right margins
- Speed View — ignores page breaks and shows your entire screenplay as if it were on a continuous scroll of paper

When you just want to focus on your screenplay without the distraction of page breaks, then you'll probably want to use Speed View. When you want to write and keep track of how each page appears, then you'll want to use Normal View. When you're polishing your screenplay and need to make sure everything looks good before you print, switch to Page View.

To see the differences between Normal View, Page View, and Speed View, follow these steps:

1. Click **View** menu and choose **Script - Normal View** (Macintosh) or click the **View** tab and click the **Normal View** icon (Windows). Final Draft displays your screenplay in Normal view. Notice that page breaks appear as horizontal lines.
2. Click **View** menu and choose **Script - Page View** (Macintosh) or click the **View** tab and click the **Page View** icon (Windows). Final Draft displays your screenplay in Page view. Notice that Final Draft displays your screenplay as it will appear when printed so you can see the margins.
3. Click **View** menu and choose **Script - Speed View** (Macintosh) or click the **View** tab and click the **Speed View** icon (Windows). Final Draft displays your screenplay in Page view. Notice that Final Draft displays your

screenplay without the distraction of page breaks or margins as shown in Figure 8-10.

All three views let you edit and read your screenplay, so just choose the view you like best and realize that you can always switch views at any time.

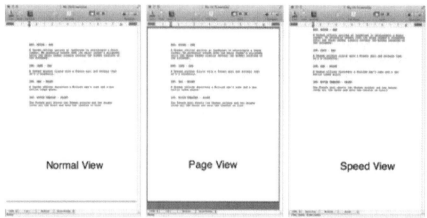

Figure 8-10. The Normal, Page, and Speed Views to display your document.

Summary

In this chapter, you learned how to write scene headings in three parts:

- Interior (INT.) or exterior (EXT.)
- A location
- A time such as DAY or NIGHT

You also learned how Final Draft's automatic formatting feature provides different styles to format your text quickly and properly. By creating scene headings, you learned how to type in Final Draft.

Once you created some scene headings in your Final Draft document, you also learned how to view your scenes as index cards that you could easily rearrange. By rearranging the order of scenes displayed as index cards, you can easily rearrange the order of scenes in your actual script.

As an alternative to displaying scenes as index cards, Final Draft can also display scenes stacked in Scene View. Like the Index Card view, Scene View lets you easily rearrange scenes by dragging them to a new location rather than cutting and pasting text to move it yourself.

Finally, you learned about the three ways to view your screenplay in Normal View, Page View, or Speed View. Speed View lets you focus on your text and nothing else. Normal View lets you see your page breaks while Page View lets you see your page breaks and the margins of your screenplay. All three views let you can edit your screenplay so choose whichever view you prefer and feel free to switch from one view to another at any time.

Save your document by pressing Command+S (Macintosh) or Ctrl+S (Windows). In the next chapter, you'll get more practice learning how to type the different parts of a properly formatted screenplay and see how Final Draft simplifies that task so you can focus on your writing.

Wallace Wang

9 UNDERSTANDING THE ELEMENTS OF A SCREENPLAY

In Chapter 8 you learned to create scene headings in the proper screenplay format. Of course, there's more to writing a scene than just defining a scene heading. The common elements of a screenplay include:

- General
- Scene heading
- Action
- Character
- Parenthetical
- Dialogue
- Transition

The four most common elements you'll use all the time are Scene headings, Action, Character, and Dialogue, so let's focus on those elements first.

Chapter 8 already explained how a Scene heading defines the location and time. Immediately following most scene headings comes an Action paragraph, which can describe the scene location in more detail and/or describe the physical movement of one or more characters.

Here are some examples of Action paragraphs after a Scene heading:

EXT. BAR - NIGHT

A broken neon sign barely hangs on the roof of a large shack otherwise known to the locals as Sherman's Bar. In front is a large gravel parking lot filled with pickup trucks, semi-trailers, and fragments of beer bottles broken and shattered from several days, maybe even months, ago.

INT. HOUSE - DAY

A paper airplane flies through the air as a swarm of kids chase after it, SCREAMING and LAUGHING. CHARLES, a middle-aged father who looks perpetually tired, gives a weak smile as he watches the kids crash into the Christmas tree.

Action paragraphs that appear right after a Scene heading can provide additional (and relevant) details important to the scene. Besides listing details that will be absolutely necessary to know later, Action paragraphs can also set the tone of the scene. Is the tone playful, forbidding, dramatic, or even humorous? Your Action paragraph can clarify this beyond the generic Scene heading.

The second purpose of Action paragraphs is to describe what characters are doing in the scene. Capitalize sounds because that makes it easy for the director to know the noises needed in that scene. When introducing a character for the first time, capitalize that character's name. Once you've introduced a character, you no longer have to capitalize that name again.

As a general rule, try to keep Action paragraphs no longer than four lines. If you need a lengthy description, break the text into two or more paragraphs. Huge chunks of text look intimidating to anyone reading your screenplay so keep your Action paragraphs as short as possible.

After Action paragraphs, the other common formatting elements are Character and Dialogue. Character defines who is speaking. The name always appears capitalized and centered in the page.

Directly underneath the character name comes that character's dialogue. There's no fixed rule for the length of a character's dialogue, but the shorter the better.

Dialogue always follows Character names such as:

> CHARLES
> Hey, kids! Go outside and play.

Sometimes after a character speaks, you can have another Action paragraph such as:

> CHARLES
> Hey, kids! Go outside and play.

SAM, Charles' 8-year old son, grabs a football off the floor and throws to Charles.

> SAM
> But it's raining outside.

Action paragraphs describe what the audience sees. Character names specify who is talking. Dialogue defines what that character says. Together with Scene headings, Action, Character, and Dialogue represent the four most common formatting elements of every screenplay.

With Action paragraphs, make sure you only describe anything a camera can see. One huge mistake novices often make is to use Action paragraphs to describe a character's thoughts or history such as the following:

> CHARLES
> Hey, kids! Go outside and play.

SAM, Charles' 8-year old son, grabs a football off the floor and throws to Charles. Sam remembers last year when his dad ignored him last Christmas and decides to get revenge.

SAM
But it's raining outside.

Notice that the Action paragraph has not only gotten wordier, but now tries to explain what a character is thinking, which no camera can possibly film. Slipping in an occasional comment to set the tone of a scene is fine, but as a general rule, if a camera can't see it, it doesn't belong in your screenplay.

Exercise #23: Typing Action, Character, and Dialogue

Just as Final Draft can automatically format Scene headings, so can Final Draft automatically format Action paragraphs, Character names and Dialogue. From Chapter 8 you learned that you can press ENTER in your script to display a popup menu of different style options such as [S] Scene Heading or [A] Action. While you can use this popup menu to choose a formatting style, Final Draft offers several shortcuts to save time.

- After you create a Scene heading and press ENTER, Final Draft automatically formats the next text as an Action paragraph.
- When the cursor appears on a new line, press TAB and Final Draft automatically formats the text as a Character name.
- After you type a Character name and press ENTER, Final Draft automatically formats the next text as Dialogue.

By providing these keystroke shortcuts, Final Draft helps you focus less on formatting your screenplay and more on writing your screenplay. To save even more time, Final Draft remembers the name of every character who has dialogue. Then as you start typing the first few letters of that character's name, Final Draft displays a popup menu of names you've already used in the past as shown in Figure 9-1.

Figure 9-1. When you start typing a Character name, Final Draft displays a SmartType menu of previously used Character names.

Now that you understand the most common formatting elements of a screenplay, let's see how to create them in Final Draft. Make sure your Final Draft document is open and follow these steps:

1. Click in the document window and move the cursor to the end of your document.
2. Press **ENTER** on the keyboard. An Elements window pops up, listing all the format styles Final Draft offers such as [A] Action or [S] Scene Heading.
3. Type **S** or use the arrow keys to highlight [S] Scene Heading and press **ENTER**.
4. Type **ext**. and press the **SPACEBAR**. Notice that as you type, Final Draft automatically capitalizes your text.
5. Type **HIGHWAY** (or any location), press the **SPACEBAR**, type -, and press the **SPACEBAR**.
6. Type **DAY**.
7. Press **ENTER**. Final Draft automatically formats the next text as an Action paragraph.
8. Type a brief description such as "All six lanes heading in one direction are jammed with cars going nowhere. MICHAEL, a teenager, opens the door to his rusted VW bug and stands on the front bumper to see how far the traffic goes."
9. Press **ENTER** and then press **TAB**. By pressing TAB,

you've told Final Draft to format the text as a Character name.

10. Type **MICHAEL** and press **ENTER**. Final Draft automatically formats the next paragraph for Dialogue.

11. Type **We'll never make it in time**. Then press **ENTER**. Final Draft automatically formats the next paragraph for Action.

As you can see, Final Draft knows which type of text typically comes next, so the program takes care of formatting your text for you. You just need to keep typing.

Exercise #24: Typing Parenthetical, Transition, and Shot Text

Although you'll always use Scene headings, Action, Character, and Dialogue, you may need to use the other formatting elements occasionally: Parenthetical, Transition, and General.

The Parenthetical always appears immediately after a Character name and is used to clarify the context or direction that the character speaks. For example, if there are three characters named Bob, Tammy, and Jonathan in a scene, you could write something like this:

JONATHAN
(whispering to Bob)
I think she just picked your pocket.

Take away this Parenthetical line and you get this:

JONATHAN
I think she just picked your pocket.

Notice with the second example, nobody knows how Jonathan says his dialogue, so it's easy to assume Jonathan simply says it to both Bob and Tammy out loud. However in the first example, the Parenthetical direction specifically tells the actor playing Jonathan how to speak the line (whisper) and who to direct the spoken words to (Bob).

Unless there's a reason for a character to speak a certain way, avoid Parenthetical directions.

The Transition format specifically defines how one scene appears after another. In most cases, the transition between one scene to another doesn't matter, but in some cases you might want to define exactly what kind of transition should take place. As you type, Final Draft tries to recognize the common transitions you might want to use. If you started typing an F or a C, Final Draft assumes you want a Fade or Cut transition as shown in Figure 9-2:

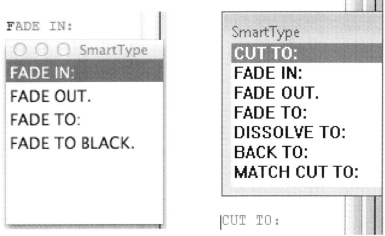

Figure 9-2. Final Draft can create common types of transitions.

If you don't like the standard transitions Final Draft provides, you can use the Transition formatting style to type your own transitions such as SMASH CUT as shown below:

JONATHAN
(whispering to Bob)
I think she just picked your pocket.

SMASH CUT:

An out of control motorcycle crashes into Tammy, sending her body flying like a rag doll through a plate glass store window that SHATTERS into a million pieces.

Like Parenthetical styles, only use Transitions when absolutely necessary. When in doubt, leave them out.

Similar to Transitions is the Shot. The Shot formatting is used to emphasize something in a scene such as highlight a character or a close up such as:

CLOSE UP

Tammy's hand deftly slips inside Bob's pants pocket and pulls out a bulging wallet.

BOB AND JONATHAN

continue walking on as if nothing happened.

JONATHAN
(whispering to Bob)
I think she just picked your pocket.

SMASH CUT:

An out of control motorcycle crashes into Tammy, sending her body flying like a rag doll through a plate glass store window that SHATTERS into a million pieces.

In this example, CLOSE UP and BOB AND JONATHAN are both formatted as Shots. Only use Shots to clarify action. Without the CLOSE UP shot, nobody knows whether it should be obvious that Tammy picked Bob's pocket or not. With the CLOSE UP shot specified, it's obvious that the audience needs to see Tammy picking the pocket.

Finally there's the General style, which can be used instead of or in addition to the Action format style to provide additional description. Remember, a screenplay is actually a recipe for a director to follow, so you must provide the bare minimum of what needs to be seen to tell your story. What you don't want to do is focus on camera angles or visual effects since that's the director's job. So you can use the General format style to clarify any part of the script that might not be clear.

To see how to use the Parenthetical and Transition formatting styles, open your Final Draft document and follow these steps:

1. Click in the document window and move the cursor to the end of your document. Make sure the cursor appears on a separate, blank line.
2. Press **ENTER** to display an Elements window and choose **[H] SHOT**.
3. Type **CLOSE UP** and press **ENTER**.
4. Type **Tammy's hand deftly slips inside Bob's pants pocket and pulls out a bulging wallet.** Press **ENTER**.
5. Press **TAB** on the keyboard, type **jonathan**, and press **ENTER**. Notice that Final Draft centers and capitalizes the character name. However, Final Draft assumes that immediately following any character name will be dialogue, so let's see how to insert a Parenthetical format underneath the character name instead.
6. Click the **Format** menu, choose **Change Element To**, and when a submenu appears, chose **Parenthetical** (Macintosh) or click the **Format** tab, click in the Elements list box and choose **Parenthetical** (Windows) as shown in Figure 9-3. As a shortcut, press **TAB** and Final Draft converts the Dialogue style to a Parenthetical style.
7. Type **whispering to Bob** within the parentheses that Final Draft has automatically inserted in your screenplay.
8. Press **ENTER**. Final Draft automatically assumes that following a Parenthetical format, you'll need to type dialogue.
9. Type **I think she just picked your pocket.**
10. Press **ENTER**. Final Draft assumes you'll next want to type an Action paragraph.

Figure 9-3. The Elements list box in the Windows version of Final Draft.

11. Click the **Format** menu, choose **Change Element To**, and when a submenu appears, chose **Transition** (Macintosh) or click the **Format** tab, click in the Elements list box and choose **Transition** (Windows). Final Draft moves the cursor to the far right of the page.
12. Type **F**. Final Draft displays a SmartType window that lists common types of transitions.
13. Use the mouse or arrow keys to select a transition, or keep typing to create your own transition and press **ENTER**.

As you can see, Final Draft can automatically format the different elements of a screenplay so you can focus on capturing your ideas as text and not be bothered with formatting your text correctly.

Exercise #25: Changing Formatted Text

Suppose you've created a screenplay, used Final Draft's automatic formatting features, and later want to change the formatting of text to a different style, such as from Character to Action?

One way to do this would be to move the cursor inside the text you want to reformat and then choose a new formatting style. On the Macintosh, you could click the **Format** menu, choose **Change Element To**, and when a submenu appears, chose a new formatting style such as **Transition**. On Windows, you could click the **Format** tab, click in the Elements list box and choose a new formatting style such as **Character**.

However, Final Draft provides a faster method known as Reformat. Instead of physically moving the cursor to a new chunk of text, the Reformat command lets Final Draft move the cursor to the next chunk of text and give you the option of choosing a new formatting style.

If you need to change the formatting of several adjacent chunks of text, the Reformat command will be faster than manually moving the cursor and choosing another formatting style.

To use the Reformat command, follow these steps:

1. Move the cursor in the text that you want to change.
2. Click the **Tools** menu and choose **Reformat** (Macintosh), or click the **Tools** tab and click the **Reformat** icon. A Reformat window appears, showing all the different formatting styles you can choose as shown in Figure 9-4.

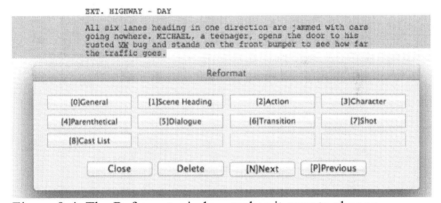

Figure 9-4. The Reformat window makes it easy to choose different formatting styles.

3. Click on the format style you want to use such as [1] Scene Heading or [5] Dialogue. (You can also type the number that represents each formatting style such as 1 for Scene Heading or 5 for Dialogue.) Final Draft changes the formatting of your text and highlights the next chunk of text.
4. Click the **Previous** button. Final Draft highlights the

previous text.
5. Click the **Next** button. Final Draft highlights the next text.
6. Click the **Close** button to make the Reformat window disappear.

The Reformat command is great when you can go through your screenplay and modify formatting styles. However, many times you may have improperly formatted text and not realize it. To help correct formatting errors, Final Draft offers a Format Assistant that can spot formatting errors and offer to fix them.

To see how the Format Assistant works, follow these steps:

1. Move the cursor to the beginning of your document and press **ENTER** to create a blank line.
2. Click the **Tools** menu and choose **Format Assistant** (Macintosh), or click the **Tools** tab and click the **Format Assistant** icon. A Format Assistant window appears, identifying possible errors and displaying formatting rules you can modify as shown in Figure 9-5.
3. Click the **Fix** button. Final Draft fixes the problem automatically.
4. Click the **Close** button. (On the Macintosh, the Close button appears as a red dot in the upper left corner of the Format Assistant window.) The Format Assistant window disappears.

The Format Assistant runs automatically before you print your screenplay. If you want to turn this feature off, click the Options button in the Format Assistant window and clear the options for checking formatting before printing.

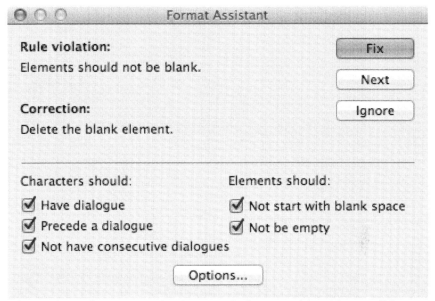

Figure 9-5. The Format Assistant window can identify possible formatting errors.

Summary

In this chapter, you learned how different screenplay elements work and the most common ones you'll use all the time. You also learned when to use Parenthetical and Transition styles (sparingly) and saw how Final Draft can automatically format text so you can focus on writing instead of formatting.

To choose a particular formatting style to use at any time, you have several options:

- At the beginning of a new line, press ENTER and when an Elements window appears, select the format style you want such as [A] Action or [C] Character.
- Click the **Format** menu, choose **Change Element To**, and when a submenu appears, chose a format style (Macintosh)
- Click on the format style label at the bottom of the document window and when a menu appears, click on a format style (Macintosh)

- Click the **Format** tab, click in the Elements list box and choose a format style (Windows)
- Press TAB to choose the Character format style
- Press TAB to convert a Dialogue format style into a Parenthetical format style
- Press ENTER to choose the default format style that typically comes next

To change formatting for text, you can use the Reformat command. To make sure your entire screenplay is correctly formatted, run the Format Assistant.

Final Draft's formatting features makes it easy to type a screenplay in the correct format. All you have to do is write a great script that creates vivid images in a reader's imagination and tells a great story that grips them from beginning to end.

While Final Draft can't do the writing for you, it can relieve you of tedious formatting chores so you can let your imagination fly.

Save your document by pressing Command+S (Macintosh) or Ctrl+S (Windows). In the next chapter, you'll learn how to further define a scene.

10 WORKING WITH SCENES

A scene defines action that happens in a single location. The beginning of a scene starts with a scene heading such as:

INT. B-2 COCKPIT— NIGHT

The end of that scene occurs at the beginning of the next scene heading. As an general rule, scenes should be short. In stage plays where set changes can be cumbersome, long scenes occur in a single location. In movies where it's easy to change locations, scenes are often far shorter.

Every scene needs to reveal at least one piece of new information that advances the story. Ideally, scenes should reveal more than one piece of new information. If the information in a scene can be revealed in another part of your screenplay, then you don't need that particular scene.

In "Terminator 2," the bad Terminator has gone to John Connor's house and taken the appearance of his step-mom. When John Connor calls, the bad Terminator mimics the step-mom's voice. When the good Terminator mimics John Connor's voice and learns that the step-mother is dead, he hangs up.

In the original screenplay for "Terminator 2," there was an extra scene where the bad Terminator kills the step-father and then explores the house, looking for clues where John Connor might go. While rummaging through John Connor's bedroom, the bad Terminator discovers letters that Sarah Connor has written to him. When the bad Terminator sees the return address on the envelope, he knows where to find John Connor.

In the movie, that entire scene got deleted because the only information that scene revealed was how the bad Terminator knows where John Connor will be. Yet after that deleted scene, John Connor tells the good Terminator that he wants to rescue his mom, but the good Terminator warns him that the bad Terminator will think of going there.

The information on where the bad Terminator can find John Connor is summed up in a single line of dialogue, completely eliminating the original scene where the bad Terminator finds Sarah Connor's address by reading it off an envelope in John Connor's bedroom.

As a general rule, the longer a scene, the more information it should reveal. Long scenes that only reveal one bit of information can often be cut or shortened. If a scene reveals one bit of information that isn't revealed elsewhere, then the scene should be as short as possible.

> Longer scenes = more information revealed
> Shorter scenes = less information revealed

Look at other screenplays and you'll see numerous scenes that got deleted from the final movie. If a scene doesn't convey new information, get rid of it. If a scene conveys information that can be revealed through another scene, get rid of the repetitive scene.

In the original screenplay for "Aliens," there's an early scene showing a family discovering the alien eggs. During this scene, the mother and father scold their children for playing in the ventilation ducts of the space base, which later explains how the little girl survived. However, this information isn't necessary so this scene wisely got eliminated.

The whole point of every scene is to advance the story and you do that by revealing new information that the audience (and the characters) didn't know before. Although scenes often tell a fragment of a story, taken together, groups of scenes (often called sequences) tell a mini-story. In every story, there are four parts:

- An attention grabber that introduces a problem and foreshadows conflict.
- A character pursuing a goal by trying to solve that problem.
- Other characters trying to foil the character from achieving a goal.
- A resolution that shows the character achieving the goal or failing to achieve the goal.

Here's how the beginning sequence from "Inglorious Basterds" works:

- The attention grabber is a dairy farmer who spots a convoy of Nazi cars heading towards his farm. (EXT. DAIRY FARM - DAY)
- The dairy farmer tries to mislead the Nazis on the whereabouts of a Jewish family. (INT. FARM HOUSE - DAY)
- The Nazi officer, known as the Jew Hunter, interrogates the dairy farmer and patiently describes the extermination of rats and the rewards that await those who help identify the location of rats.
- The dairy farmer points to the direction of where the Jewish family is hiding under the floors, and the Nazi officer orders his men to machine gun the area. (EXT. DAIRY FARM -DAY) Miraculously, a girl escapes and flees as the Nazi officer taunts her.

Sequences must begin by grabbing our attention with a problem. At first, we may not know what this problem might be, but we do know that it hints of future conflict, which keeps us wanting to know more.

Second, we learn the goals of the opposing characters. One character is trying to pursue a goal and another character is trying to foil that goal. Initially, it looks like the character pursuing the goal will succeed.

Third, the character opposing the goal seems to gain the advantage and looks like he or she will foil the goal.

Fourth, the goal either gets resolved or not with one character the winner and the other the loser. Then the sequence ends with a cliffhanger to lead us directly into the next sequence by posing an unanswered question. In the opening sequence of "Inglorious Basterds," the cliffhanger is what will happen to the surviving girl?

Reveal the most information possible in scenes that are as short as possible, and that will go a long way towards creating an interesting movie.

Exercise #26: Defining a Scene with Titles, Colors, and Summaries

Every scene needs a purpose by revealing more information about your story. A sequence of scenes collectively tell a mini-story. To help you define the purpose of each scene, Final Draft lets you define the following additional information about your scenes to help you stay focused:

- Title
- Color
- Summary

Just as your screenplay title can help you stay focused on your overall story, so can scene titles help remind you of the purpose of each scene. Scene titles are separate from scene headings and won't print out with your actual screenplay.

Final Draft lets you color code your scenes. That way you can use

Red to identify scenes involving the villain and Green to identify scenes invoking the hero. Now by browsing through your list of scenes, you can quickly see whether you have too many scenes on one character while ignoring other characters for too long.

A summary lets you describe the scene's action without actually writing the complete scene in screenplay format. By creating a summary, you can quickly define what happens in each scene. When you're happy with your summary of a scene, then you can write the screenplay directions for that scene.

If you start writing a scene without knowing its purpose, you'll likely forget to include vital information, fail to make the scene serve its purpose in advancing the story, or write irrelevant information that will have to be dumped later. You don't want to rush into writing your screenplay too soon. Planning ahead is almost always a better option than rushing ahead, winding up in a dead end, and not knowing how to get back out again without deleting everything you just wrote.

Let's see how Final Draft makes it easy to store additional information about a scene. First, practice writing some dialogue and some descriptive actions for at least one of your scenes. When you have short dialogue between two characters, along with descriptive actions, follow these steps:

1. Move the cursor anywhere in the text of the scene you just wrote.
2. Click the **Edit** menu and choose **Select Scene** (Macintosh) or click the **Edit** tab and click the **Select Scene** icon (Windows). Final Draft highlights the entire scene so you can see it easily as shown in Figure 10-1.
3. If the Navigator window isn't visible, click the **Tools** menu and choose **Show Navigator** (Macintosh) or click the **Tools** tab and click the **Show Navigator** icon (Windows). The Navigator window appears.
4. Click the **Scenes** tab in the Navigator window. Final Draft displays a list of scenes at the top of the Navigator window and the details of the currently selected scene at the bottom

of the Navigator window as shown in Figure 10-2.

```
INT. CAFE - DAY

A German soldier flirts with a French girl and reveals that
he's a celebrity.


INT. BAR - NIGHT

A German officer discovers a British spy's ruse and a gun
battle takes place.


INT. MOVIE THEATER - NIGHT

The French girl shoots the German soldier and her helper
locks all the doors and sets the theater on fire.


EXT. HIGHWAY - DAY

All six lanes heading in one direction are jammed with cars
going nowhere. MICHAEL, a teenager, opens the door to his
rusted VW bug and stands on the front bumper to see how far
the traffic goes.

                    MICHAEL
          We'll never make it in time.

                    SALLY
          Can we just drive over the median
          and get out of the road altogether?

Michael looks around. No cars are moving anywhere.

                    MICHAEL
          Must be an accident somewhere,
          although I don't know what kind of
          accident could stop traffic on both
          sides of the freeway.
```

Figure 10-1. The Select Scene command highlights a single scene.

With the Scenes tab selected in the Navigator window, you can see the order of your scenes and the page numbers where each scene begins. If you want, you can also identify one or more scenes with a Title and a Color.

Neither the Title nor the Color will appear when you print your screenplay. Both the Title and Color are solely to help you identify and group related scenes together. For example, you could use the color Red to identify all scenes that involves your villain. Titles just give you a way to identify certain scenes that make sense to you, such as referring to one scene as "The Bar Battle" scene and another scene "The Car Crash" scene.

To give a scene a Title and/or Color, make sure the Navigator window displays the Scenes tab and then follow these steps:

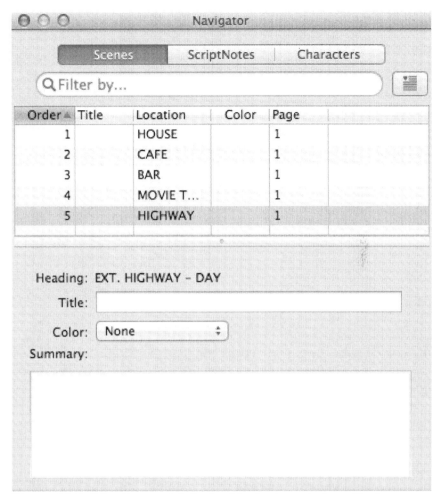

Figure 10-2. The Scenes tab in the Navigator window displays your list of scenes.

1. Click in the **Title** text box and type a descriptive title for your scene.
2. Click in the **Color** popup menu and choose a color to identify your scene. Color codes are completely arbitrary so just decide what you want each color to represent and use that color coding consistently.
3. Click in the **Summary** text box and type a description of the scene, what type of information the scene needs to reveal, how this scene relates to another scene, etc. Like a

Title, the scene Summary exists solely for your arbitrary use so use it anyway you like.

When you finish adding a Title and Color to a scene, the Scenes tab in the Navigator window displays your added information.

Tip: You can change the width of the Navigator window by moving the mouse pointer over the right edge of the Navigator window and dragging the mouse left or right.

Exercise #27: Tracking Character Changes in Scenes

In most scenes, two or more characters are both pursuing goals of their own that involve the other character. This pursuit of multiple goals by multiple characters in a scene creates conflict, which makes the scene interesting while also providing us with additional information.

In "The Hunger Games," the hero has to demonstrate her skills so the game judges can rate her on a scale of 1 to 12 so bettors can place odds on a likely winner. The hero's initial goal is to demonstrate her skill. When she shoots an arrow and misses her target, the judges lose interest in her.

Quickly, she shoots a second arrow and hits her target dead on, but by now the judges haven't even noticed. To overcome this problem of being ignored, the hero aims an arrow at an apple in a pig's mouth that the judges are eating. Suddenly when the judges see that she hit the apple perfectly, their shocked looks show that the hero has finally achieved her initial goal, which was to make a good impression.

A good scene (or sequence of scenes) always tells a mini-story like this:

- One character has a goal
- A second character blocks that goal
- The first character finds a way to overcome that obstacle

- The first character either gets or fails to achieve that goal

At the end of every scene, something has changed. In this scene from "The Hunger Games," the judges' impression of the hero has gone from benign neglect to shocked admiration.

Watch bad movies and you'll see mistakes with scenes. One common mistake is that nobody in the scene has a goal of any kind, so the action is entirely meaningless. A second common mistake is that one character has a goal and achieves it with no obstacles in the way. Without conflict, there's no action and without action, there's no story.

What every scene needs is conflict and surprise. We need conflict to cause problems for the main character of that scene. We need surprise to keep the scene from being predictable.

In "The Hunger Games" scene, what would have happened if the hero had shot her arrow, hit her target, and the judges were impressed? There would be no conflict and the scene would feel deadly dull. When the hero faces an obstacle, she finds a surprising way to overcome that problem, and that surprise is what keeps the scene fresh and memorable.

At the end of every scene, something must change for better or worse. By mixing the outcome of scenes, you take your audience on an emotional roller coaster ride where sometimes the hero's life seems better and sometimes it seems worse.

Another scene in "The Hunger Games" occurs when the hero strays too close to the border of the games arena. To drive her back to the center, the games makers light the forest on fire, forcing the hero to run. To make her problem even worse, they shoot fireballs at her, badly burning her leg. By the time the hero escapes from the forest, she's still alive, but in worse shape than before.

You don't want too many scenes together where the outcome is always good or always bad for the hero. Just like a roller coaster is more fun when it constantly goes up and down, so will your story be far more interesting when the outcomes of your scenes alternate from good to bad.

You might have two scenes, back to back, where the outcome is good for your hero. Then suddenly the next scene creates a bad outcome. There are no set rules for alternating the outcome of your scenes, but too many good or bad outcomes in a row starts making your story predictable and predictable stories get boring.

To help you identify the change for the characters in every scene, Final Draft lets you store the character's change known as the Character Arc Beat. This lets you define the following for each character:

- The character's goal for that scene
- The obstacles facing each character
- The solution each character tries to overcome that obstacle
- The final outcome (good or bad).

When you have two or more characters in a scene, one character will achieve the initial goal but the other character may not. In "The Sixth Sense," there's a scene where the hero waits for a little boy to come home. When the little boy sees the hero in his living room, the hero tries to gain the boy's trust by playing a guessing game. Initially, that works, but then he starts guessing wrong and the little boy flees. The hero's character arc beat might look like this:

- Gain the trust of the little boy
- The boy is reluctant to talk to him
- Play a guessing game
- Too many wrong guesses causes the boy to flee

In that same scene, the little boy has his own character arc beat that looks like this:

- Get away from the hero

- The hero keeps talking to him and offers to play a guessing game to get information out of him
- The boy plays the guessing game
- The hero guesses wrong too many times, giving the boy a reason to escape

When characters in a scene pursue multiple goals, that scene feels more realistic. When characters don't have any goal of their own to pursue, those characters feel pointless and the entire scene feels less engaging. We care about what happens to people who we know. We don't care about people we don't know. By giving each character a goal, we can relate to that character as a real person.

To see how to define a character's changes in a scene, make sure the Navigator window appears and then follow these steps:

1. Click the **Characters** tab in the Navigator window. Final Draft displays a list of characters in the currently selected scene as shown in Figure 10-3.
2. Click on a character name in the **Characters in this scene** box. (If you click the plus sign, you can add a character name. If you select a character name and click the minus sign, you can remove a character name from this list.)
3. Click in the **Character Arc Beat** text box and type the initial goal of the character in that scene.
4. Type a second paragraph that describes the obstacles that character faces in that scene.
5. Type a third paragraph that describes the solution that character chooses to overcome the obstacle.
6. Type a fourth paragraph that describes the outcome for that character, either good or bad.
7. Repeat steps 2-6 for each character in that scene.

Every character in a scene should have a goal of some kind. The more important that character, the more important that goal. Even minor characters need goals to make their behavior more realistic.

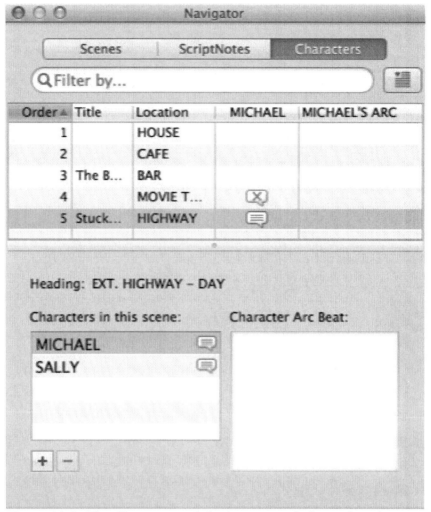

Figure 10-3. The Characters tab lets you store information about how each character changes in the scene.

In the original "Robocop," there's a scene where a man robs a gas station and holds a gun at the face of the scared cashier. The cashier's goal at that point is to avoid getting killed, so he cooperates. Since the cashier is a minor character, he has a minor goal, but knowing this minor goal insures that his actions remain consistent with his goals.

If the cashier's goal was to avoid getting killed, suddenly having him pull out a hidden gun and shoot the robber in the face might be one solution, but it's an unlikely one for such a minor character. Just having the cashier be scared enough to hand over the cash is consistent with that character's minor goal.

By knowing each character's goals in a scene, you can later write that scene and keep your scene consistent with the character arc beat you wrote down. If you feel compelled to write something different than your character arc beat, ask yourself why?

You might have a better idea, or you might be straying from your scene's purpose. Either way, the written character arc beat can help you evaluate your scene when you finally write it.

Summary

In this chapter, you learned how to structure a scene, how to select an entire scene in Final Draft, how to create and store a Title, Color code, and Summary for each scene, and how to define character arc beats for each character in a scene.

Make sure you know how to open, move, and resize Final Draft's Navigator window. The Scenes tab and the Characters tab let you store information about your different scenes. That way you can type your screenplay and refer to your notes about each scene and character.

Save your document by pressing Command+S (Macintosh) or Ctrl+S (Windows). In the next chapter, you'll learn more about working with the characters in your screenplay.

Wallace Wang

11 MAKING DIALOGUE COME TO LIFE

Although dialogue is the most common element of a screenplay, novice screenwriters often reveal too much information through dialogue. The problem is that hearing someone describe something is far less interesting than seeing them reveal their true feelings. To learn how to tell a story only through visuals, the two best movies to watch are "WALL-E" and "The Artist."

In "WALL-E," notice how much you can learn about what WALL-E wants and his personality just by watching him rummage through a garbage dump. Without a single line of dialogue, you can see that WALL-E is curious, playful, caring, and lonely.

In "The Artist," a young woman is in love with a silent screen star. Instead of just saying she loves the silent screen star, she sneaks into his dressing room, hugs his jacket hanging on a post, and slip her arm through the sleeve to make believe his arm is holding and caressing her. That scene alone is more than enough to imprint in our minds how much she really loves him.

Later there's a scene where the silent screen star survives a fire in his house and the doctors tell the young woman that they found him clutching a movie reel. When she opens the movie reel can and looks at the film, she sees it contains an early scene when the two of them were dancing and laughing together while making a movie.

The fact that the silent screen star clung to that particular movie reel and she sees the scene that he saved reveals his love for her too. All that information and emotion gets imparted to us through visuals alone with no dialogue whatsoever.

Study "The Artist" for how sparsely dialogue needs to be revealed on the screen. Another scene shows the silent screen star looking at a tuxedo in a store window, although he can no longer afford it. To show his longing, the movie shows him studying his reflection in the store window glass, seeing how the tuxedo would look on him.

By creating visually interesting scenes, you can tell much of your story without any dialogue. Then use dialogue only when absolutely necessary. As an exercise, see how much of your screenplay you can tell through visuals alone. Then if you absolutely cannot think of a way to reveal information visually, think of a way to reveal it through interesting dialogue.

Watch any Quentin Tarantino film to study how dialogue can be both fascinating and revealing while subtly setting up story elements in seemingly harmless conversation. Remember, every action, speech, and visual must be interesting and different to move the story along. The more your story's actions can reveal, the faster your audience will follow the story. Often times silence can the best way to reveal the true emotions of your characters.

Silent movies display dialogue sparingly because movie goers want to watch a movie, not read words on a screen. Similarly, today's movie goers want to watch a movie, not listen to speech. Of course, when speech is the best way to convey information quickly, then you need to know how to write dialogue.

Final Draft can help you write and format dialogue correctly. However, you still need to learn to write lean, sparse dialogue. As with all types of writing, try to convey as much information as possible using as few words as possible.

In screenplays, dialogue represents the illusion of real speech. Listen to ordinary people talking and you'll hear lots of greetings, shortcuts, slang, and roundabout discussions. All this must be cut ruthlessly from your screenplay. In the illusionary world of movies, characters speak efficiently.

The criteria for any dialogue involves checking the following:

- Is it necessary? If you can take out the dialogue and not affect comprehension, the dialogue is not needed.
- Does it reveal necessary information? Dialogue often reveals the personality of characters by what they say, how they say it, and who they talk to. Dialogue can also introduce new information that will play a crucial role in the story later on.
- Does it show us something new or different? Dialogue must always show us something new or something familiar from another perspective. If dialogue repeats what we already know, it's not needed.
- Is it unique to that character? Novice screenwriters often write dialogue that sounds like the screenwriter. Vary the word length, word choice, and sentence pattern because a Harvard professor with a Ph.D. in French literature will likely speak and think differently than a tobacco farmer living in North Carolina during the Civil War.

Perhaps the biggest trap in writing dialogue involves creating distinct voices. It's easy to write dialogue so that every character sounds alike. Initially, just worry about getting your thoughts down. You can always edit dialogue later.

Once you've captured dialogue for your characters in a scene, make sure it's consistent with both that particular character and with other dialogue spoken by that character in other scenes. Then edit the dialogue so the dialogue sounds like it could only come out of that particular character.

Think of how different Ron Burgundy sounds in "Anchorman" compared to the Terminator in "Terminator 2" or even how distinct Thelma's dialogue sounds compared to Louise's in "Thelma and Louise." Even if their dialogue conveys the same meaning, the words they use will be subtly or noticeably different.

Exercise #28: Listening to Dialogue

To help you create distinctive dialogue for all your characters, Final Draft lets you assign computer-generated voices to each of your characters. By hearing your dialogue spoken out loud, you can listen for awkward word choices and phrases that aren't distinctive enough to that character.

First, you need to assign a computer-generated voice to each of your characters. You can adjust this voice by changing its speed and pitch if you want, or just use the voice as is. After you've assigned a specific type of voice to a character, you can have Final Draft read your dialogue.

To assign voices to a character, make sure you've written some dialogue for at least two characters. Then follow these steps:

1. Click the **Tools** menu and choose **Assign Voices** (Macintosh) or click the **Tools** tab and click the **Assign Voices** icon (Windows). An Assign Voices window appears.
2. Click the **Characters** tab to view your list of character names as shown in Figure 11-1.
3. Click on a character name listed in the **Characters** box.
4. Click on a name listed in the **Actors** box such as Old Man or Woman 2. You may want to click the **Preview** button to hear a sample of your chosen computer-generated voice.
5. Click **OK** to assign that voice to that character. Repeat this step for each character.

In case you don't quite like the way each computer-generated voice sounds, you can modify the pitch and speed.

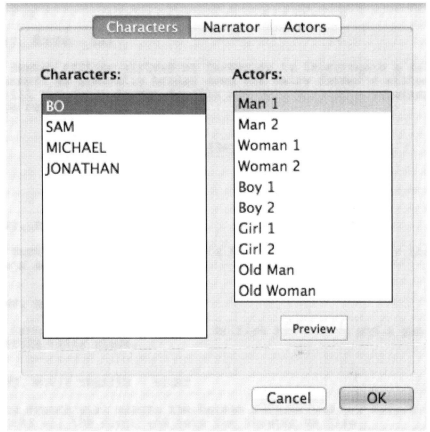

Figure 11-1. The Characters tab in the Assign Voices window lets you assign a voice to each character.

To chance a computer-generated voice, follow these steps:

1. Click the **Tools** menu and choose **Assign Voices** (Macintosh) or click the **Tools** tab and click the **Assign Voices** icon (Windows). An Assign Voices window appears.
2. Click the **Actors** tab to view the list of available computer-generated voices as shown in Figure 11-2.

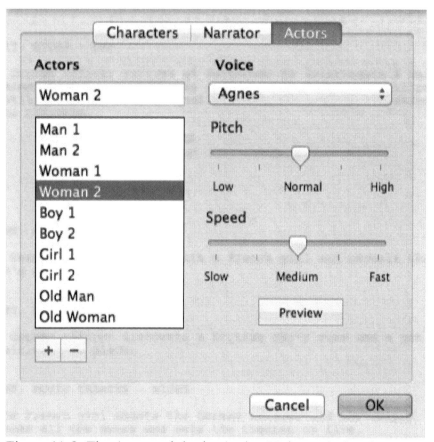

Figure 11-2. The Actors tab in the Assign Voices window lets you modify the computer-generated voices.

3. Click on an actor name in the **Actors** box such as Old Woman or Man 2.
4. Click in the **Voices** popup menu and choose a different type of voice.
5. (Optional) Drag the **Pitch** and **Speed** sliders.
6. Click the **Preview** button to hear how the voice sounds.
7. Click **OK** to save your changes or click **Cancel** to discard your changes.

Finally, you can define a narrator's voice who can speak everything in your screenplay except dialogue. This can be handy in listening to your description of scenes, but if you don't want to hear the computer recite every scene heading, transition line, or character name, you can modify the behavior of the narrator by following these steps:

1. Click the **Tools** menu and choose **Assign Voices** (Macintosh) or click the **Tools** tab and click the **Assign Voices** icon (Windows). An Assign Voices window appears.
2. Click the **Narrator** tab to view the list of available computer-generated voices as shown in Figure 11-3.

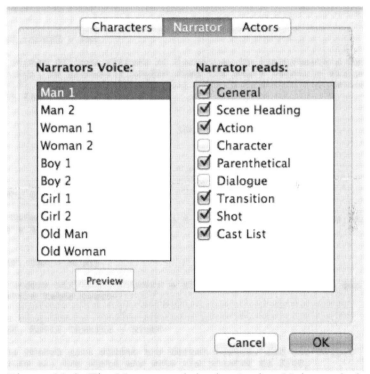

Figure 11-3. The Narrator tab in the Assign Voices window.

1. Click on a voice to use for your narrator in the **Narrator voice** box such as Man 1 or Girl 2.
2. Select (or clear) the check boxes in the **Narrator reads** box. If you want the narrator to read scene headings, then put a check mark in the Scene Heading check box. If you leave a check box blank, the narrator won't read that text.

3. Click **OK**.

Once you've assigned voices to your characters and chosen a voice for your narrator, along with defining which items to read, you're ready to listen to Final Draft read your screenplay out loud.

To make Final Draft read your screenplay, follow these steps:

1. Move the cursor to the part of your screenplay where you want Final Draft to start reading your text out loud.
2. Click the **Tools** menu and choose **Speech Control**. A Speech Control window appears. (Macintosh) Or click the **Tools** tab (Windows).
3. Click the **Play** button.
4. Click the **Stop** button any time you want Final Draft to stop reading your screenplay.

Two other buttons you can click include:

*   Rewind - Moves back to read the previous part of your screenplay so you can hear it again
*   Fast Forward - Skips over the current part of your screenplay to the next element.

Exercise #29: Highlighting and Replacing Character Names

Listening to your dialogue spoken out loud can help you hear if your dialogue is distinct enough. Another way to examine your dialogue is to read it. To make it easy to spot dialogue from certain characters, Final Draft can automatically highlight dialogue in different colors.

For example, if you had a character named Michael and another character named Sally, you could have Final Draft highlight all of Michael's dialogue in red or all of Sally's dialogue in green. That way you could easily focus on just one character's dialogue to make sure it sounds right.

To highlight character names and dialogue, make sure your screenplay contains character names and dialogue, then follow these steps:

1. Click the **Format** menu and choose **Highlight Characters** (Macintosh), or click the **Format** tab and click the **Highlight Characters** icon (Windows). A Highlight Characters window appears as shown in Figure 11-4.

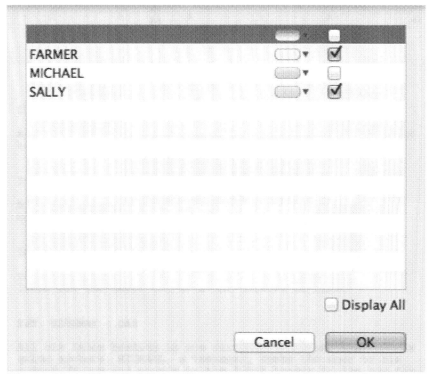

Figure 11-4. The Highlight Characters window lets you choose a color for each character.

2. Click in the color popup menu to the right of a character name. When a popup menu appears, click on a color such as Blue or Yellow.
3. Select (or clear) the check box that appears to the far right. If the check box is selected, Final Draft highlights your chosen character's name and dialogue throughout your screenplay. (You can click the **Display All** check box to

select or clear all character names at once.)

4. Click **OK**. Final Draft highlights your characters in your chosen colors as shown in Figure 11-5.

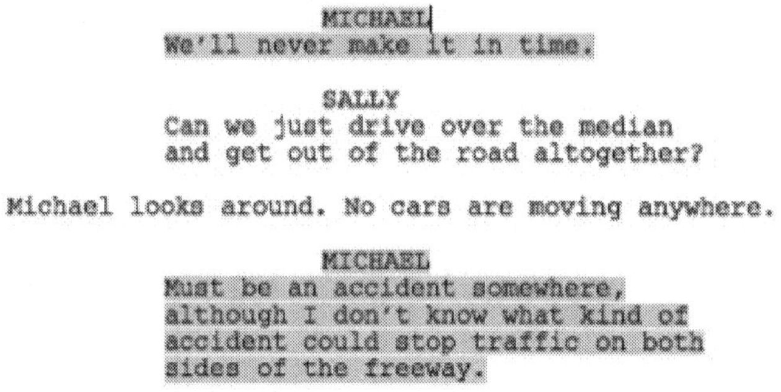

```
                    MICHAEL
We'll never make it in time.

                    SALLY
Can we just drive over the median
and get out of the road altogether?

Michael looks around. No cars are moving anywhere.

                    MICHAEL
Must be an accident somewhere,
although I don't know what kind of
accident could stop traffic on both
sides of the freeway.
```

Figure 11-5. Final Draft can highlight character names and dialogue.

When you type character names and their dialogue in your screenplay, you'll likely run into two problems. First, if you suddenly decide to change the name of a character, you don't want to replace the character's name yourself through all 120 pages of your screenplay. Second, if you accidentally misspell the name of a character, Final Draft will think this misspelling is actually another character name. Let's see how to fix both problems.

To make it easy to search and replace just character names in a screenplay, Final Draft offers a Replace Character command. Unlike ordinary search and replace commands in other word processors, Final Draft's Replace Character command will only focus on replacing text formatted with the Character style. Other word processors simply search and replace text throughout your document, which can often mean accidentally changing text that shouldn't be changed.

To change a character's name throughout your screenplay, follow these steps:

1. Click the **Edit** menu and choose **Replace Character** (Macintosh), or click the **Edit** tab and click the **Replace**

Character icon (Windows). A Replace Character dialog box appears as shown in Figure 11-6.

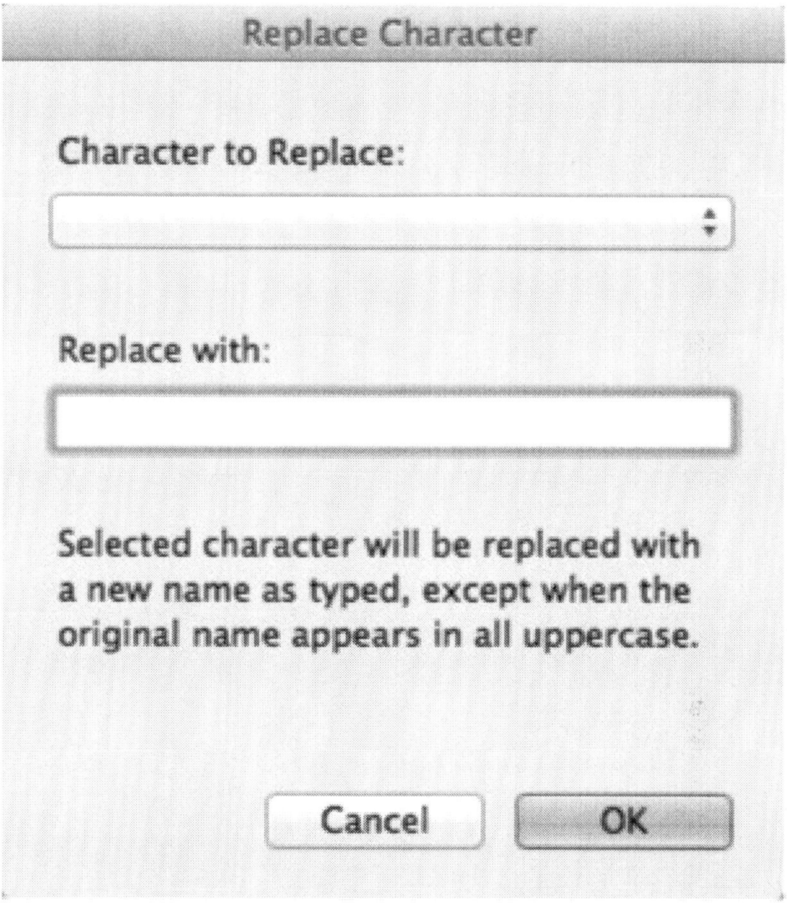

Replace Character

Character to Replace:

Replace with:

Selected character will be replaced with a new name as typed, except when the original name appears in all uppercase.

Cancel   OK

Figure 11-6. The Replace Character dialog box lets you choose a character name to change.

2. Click in the **Character to Replace** popup menu and choose the character name you want to change.
3. Click in the **Replace with** text box and type the new name you want for that character.
4. Click **OK**. Final Draft changes your character name throughout your screenplay.

If you misspelled a character name, Final Draft will save that misspelled name. Then each time you type that character's name, Final Draft will display the correct spelling along with the misspelled version.

Obviously, this can get annoying so to delete the misspelled character name, follow these steps:

1. Click the **Document** menu and choose **SmartType** (Macintosh), or click the **Document** tab and click the **SmartType** icon (Windows). A SmartType dialog box appears as shown in Figure 11-7.

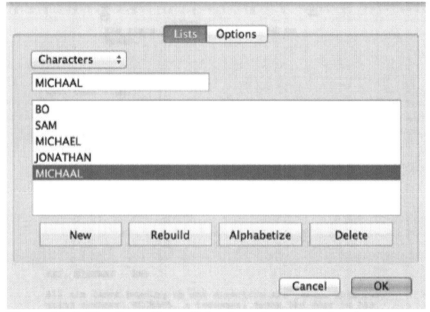

Figure 11-7. The SmartType dialog box that stores the character names you've used.

2. Click on the misspelled character name you want to delete.
3. Click **Delete**.
4. Click **OK**.

After you've deleted a misspelled character name from SmartType, use the Replace Character command to replace the misspelled name with the correct spelling. That way you'll also fix any misspellings still in your screenplay.

Exercise #30: Creating Dual Dialogue

Most of the time one character speaks and then another character follows. Sometimes the dialogue may slightly overlap, but most of the time, only one character speaks at a time.

However, sometimes you may want two characters to speak at once. To specify this in a screenplay, you need to type the character names and dialogue side by side as shown in Figure 11-8.

```
EXT. HIGHWAY - DAY

All six lanes heading in one direction are jammed with cars
going nowhere. MICHAEL, a teenager, opens the door to his
rusted VW bug and stands on the front bumper to see how far
the traffic goes. SALLY sits in the passenger seat, playing
with her phone.
                MICHAEL                      SALLY
We'll never make it in time.    Can we just drive over the
                                median and get out of the
                                road altogether?
```

Figure 11-8. Dual dialogue displays character dialogue side by side.

To create dual dialogue, follow these steps:

1. Move the cursor to one character's dialogue, making sure that a second character's dialogue immediately follows.
2. Click the **Format** menu and choose **Dual Dialogue** (Macintosh), or click the **Format** tab and click the **Dual Dialogue** icon. Final Draft displays your dialogue side by side.

Any time you want to convert dual dialogue back to regular dialogue, just move the cursor inside the dual dialogue and choose the Dual Dialogue command again.

Summary

In this chapter, you learned how to make Final Draft read your screenplay out loud so you can listen to your characters' dialogue. In addition, you learned how to highlight character names and dialogue in your screenplay and how to replace character names without affecting the rest of your screenplay by mistake.

In those rare cases when you need characters to speak simultaneously, you also learned how to use Final Draft's dual dialogue feature.

Dialogue should convey information to the audience that can't be presented any other way. Ideally, try to tell your story while avoiding dialogue as much as possible, much like how silent movies limited actual dialogue to avoid forcing the audience to read too often. By telling your story visually without relying on dialogue too heavily, you can tell your story more effectively.

Save your document by pressing Command+S (Macintosh) or Ctrl+S (Windows). In the next chapter, you'll learn how to edit your screenplay in Final Draft.

12 EDITING A SCREENPLAY

Nobody writes a perfect screenplay the first time. If you search the Internet, you can find plenty of screenplays of famous movies. By reading the original screenplay and comparing it to the final movie, you can see which scenes got modified, which scenes got rearranged, and which scenes got eliminated altogether.

Rather than worry about creating a perfect screenplay the first time you write it, plan on revising it at least one more time, most likely several more times. Each time you edit your screenplay, focus on a different element such as focusing on the hero's story on the first reading, focusing on the villain's story on the second reading, focusing on the secondary characters' subplots on the third reading, and so on.

You want to create a finished screenplay as quickly as possible, but you also want to create the best screenplay, which means taking time to revise it until it's the best it can be. It does you no good to send people a lousy screenplay quickly. You want to send them the best screenplay you can write, so take your time.

To help you edit a screenplay, Final Draft provides several features:

- Split views
- ScriptNotes
- Revisions

Split views let you see two parts of the same screenplay on the screen at once. That way you can edit the beginning while viewing the end (or vice versa).

ScriptNotes are actual notes you can attach to specific parts of your screenplay. For example, you might want to revise a specific character's dialogue so you could attach a ScriptNote to that dialogue, write down some ideas for fixing it, and come back to it at a later time. Think of a ScriptNote like sticking a paperclip or sticky note on a page of a screenplay.

Revisions let you color code your changes so people can see which pages you modified or added. The first revisions might appear in blue, the second revisions might appear in red, and so on. If you look at actual shooting scripts, you'll find a screenplay filled with different color pages.

Exercise #31: Split Views to Look at Different Parts of a Screenplay Simultaneously

Split views let you see two separate parts of your screenplay at the same time. That way you can view and edit scenes that may not be adjacent. For example, the end of your screenplay might require a character to have a hammer, so you may need to edit a middle scene to make sure that character grabs a hammer.

Final Draft can split your screenplay in half vertically or horizontally. Depending on how large your screen might be, you might prefer one type of split over the other.

To split a screenplay, follow these steps:

1. Click the View menu and choose Split Vertically or Split Horizontally (Macintosh) or click the View tab and click the Split Vertically or Split Horizontally icon (Windows). Final Draft displays your screenplay in two panels.
2. Click in one panel and scroll up or down. Notice that Final Draft lets you scroll in one pane without affecting the other pane.
3. Move the mouse pointer over the Split bar (it looks like a gray border) separating the two panels as shown in Figure

12-1.

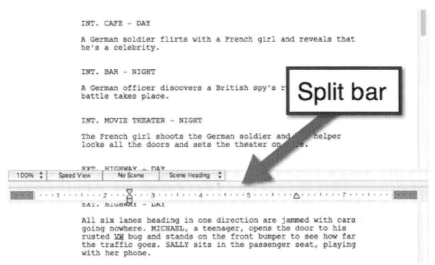

Figure 12-1. A Split bar separates the two panels.

4. Drag the Split bar to resize the two panels.
5. Click the View menu and choose Swap Panels (Macintosh) or click the View tab and click the Swap Panels icon (Windows). Final Draft switches the parts of the screenplay in each panel to the other one.
6. Click the View menu and choose Unsplit Panels (Macintosh) or click the View tab and click the Unsplit Panels icon (Windows). Final Draft displays your screenplay in one window again.

In case you find split views too tiny and cramped, you can also make a copy of your screenplay and view the copy in a second window. The drawback with this technique is that you have to make sure you restrict any changes to a single document or else you risk making multiple changes to separate files and not know which changes belong where.

Exercise #32: Using ScriptNotes

If you're quickly skimming through your screenplay, you might spot certain scenes that you'd like to review later. With printed screenplays, you can scribble a note on that page. With Final Draft, you can attach a ScriptNote and type text to yourself, such as ideas for modifying that particular spot.

ScriptNotes are similar to General Notes. The main difference is that a ScriptNote attaches itself to a specific spot in your screenplay while a General Note does not.

To create a ScriptNote, follow these steps:

1. Move the cursor where you want to place a ScriptNote.
2. Click the Insert menu and choose ScriptNote (Macintosh) or click the Insert tab and click the ScriptNote icon. Final Draft displays a tiny flag in the right margin of your screenplay and displays a blank ScriptNote in the Navigator window as shown in Figure 12-2.

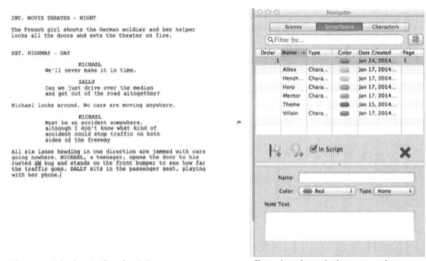

Figure 12-2. A ScriptNote appears as a flag in the right margin.

3. Click in the Name text box and type a descriptive name for your ScriptNote.
4. Click in the Color popup menu and choose a color to associate with your ScriptNote, such as yellow for changes involving a secondary character.
5. (Optional) Click in the Type popup menu and when a menu

      appears, choose New Type and type a descriptive category
      for your ScriptNote.

6. Click in the Note Text box and type text for your note.

Once you've inserted a ScriptNote in your screenplay, you can always view it again by following these steps:

1. Make sure the Navigator window is open and click on the ScriptNotes tab. Final Draft displays a list of ScriptNotes and General Notes.
2. Double-click on a ScriptNote. Final Draft displays the text of that ScriptNote and also displays the page where you inserted the ScriptNote.

Remember: To remove a ScriptNote (or General Note), click on the note in the Navigator window and click the **Remove** icon (it looks like a big red X).

Exercise #33: Tracking Revisions

No matter how many times you may revise your screenplay, you'll likely need to make changes for other people. To identify which parts of your screenplay you changed, Final Draft displays a vertical row of asterisks in the right margin as shown in Figure 12-3.

```
All six lanes heading in one direction are jammed with cars
going nowhere. MICHAEL, a teenager, opens the door to his
rusted VW bug and stands on the front bumper to see how far
the traffic goes. SALLY sits in the passenger seat, playing
with her phone while Bo, Sally's little sister sits in the      *
back seat.                                                      *

                        BO                                      *
            So how much longer will we have to                  *
            sit here?                                           *

Bo stares out the window.                                       *
```

Figure 12-3. Final Draft can identify changes in a screenplay with a vertical row of asterisks.

To make it easy to see which pages you revised, Final Draft can also display headers on each revised page. Hollywood often prints revised pages on different color paper, so Final Draft can print a header on revised pages listing Blue Rev. or Pink Rev. in case you don't have any colored paper for your printer.

To track revisions, you must turn Final Draft's revision feature on by following these steps:

1. Click the Production menu and choose Revisions (Macintosh) or click the Production tab and click the Revisions Setup icon (Windows). A Revisions dialog box appears as shown in Figure 12-4.

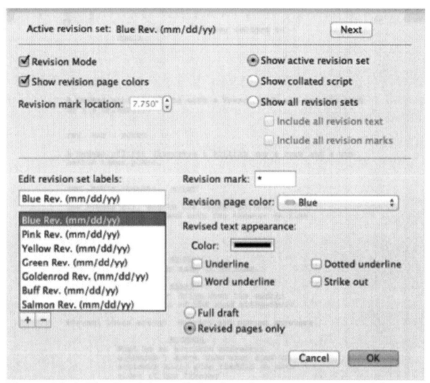

Figure 12-4. The Revisions dialog box lets you turn on revisions.

2. Click on the Revision Mode check box to select it.
3. Click on the Show revision page colors check box to select it (if you want Final Draft to display a revision header on

each revised page).

4. (Windows only) Click the Revision sets button to open a Revision Sets dialog box as shown in Figure 12-5.
5. Click on a revision label in the Edit revision set labels box.
6. (Optional) Make any other changes you want such as typing a different revision mark (instead of an asterisk) or choosing a different color for revised text such as green.
7. Click OK. (Windows users need to click OK a second time.) Now when you add or delete text in your screenplay, Final Draft will add the revision marks in the right margin and display a revision label at the top of each revised page.

To turn off revision marks, just clear the **Revision Mode** and **Show revision page colors** check boxes.

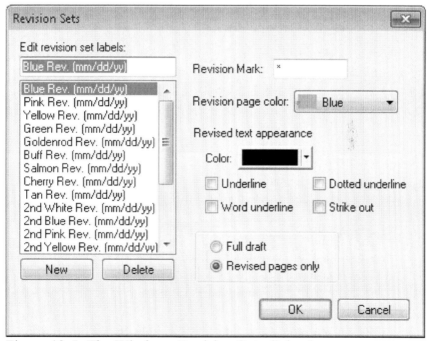

Figure 12-5. The Windows Revision Sets dialog box.

If you want to selectively remove revision marks from a screenplay, follow these steps:

1. Highlight the text that contains revision marks in the right margin.
2. Click the Production menu and choose Clear Revised (Macintosh) or click the Production tab and click the Clear Revised icon (Windows). Final Draft removes revision marks.

Tip: If you click on the **Production** menu and choose **Mark Revised** (Macintosh) or click the Production tab and click on the **Mark** Revised icon (Windows), you can manually add revision marks to any part of your screenplay without going through the hassle of turning on revision marks.

Revision marks make it easy to see what changes you or someone else made to a screenplay. Ideally, you should only make changes on a single file. Realistically, you'll wind up making copies of a file, sending them to different people, and then wind up with a bunch of different files that have been modified by other people.

In the old days, you would have to examine each file to look for changes, but Final Draft can simplify this process by merging two files and showing you the differences between them. To compare two versions of the same screenplay, follow these steps:

1. Open the first version of your screenplay.
2. Click the Tools menu and choose Script Compare (Macintosh) or click the Tools tab and click the Script Compare icon (Windows). An Open dialog box appears.
3. Click on a second version of your screenplay and click Compare/Open. Final Draft shows the changes between the two screenplays as shown in Figure 12-6.

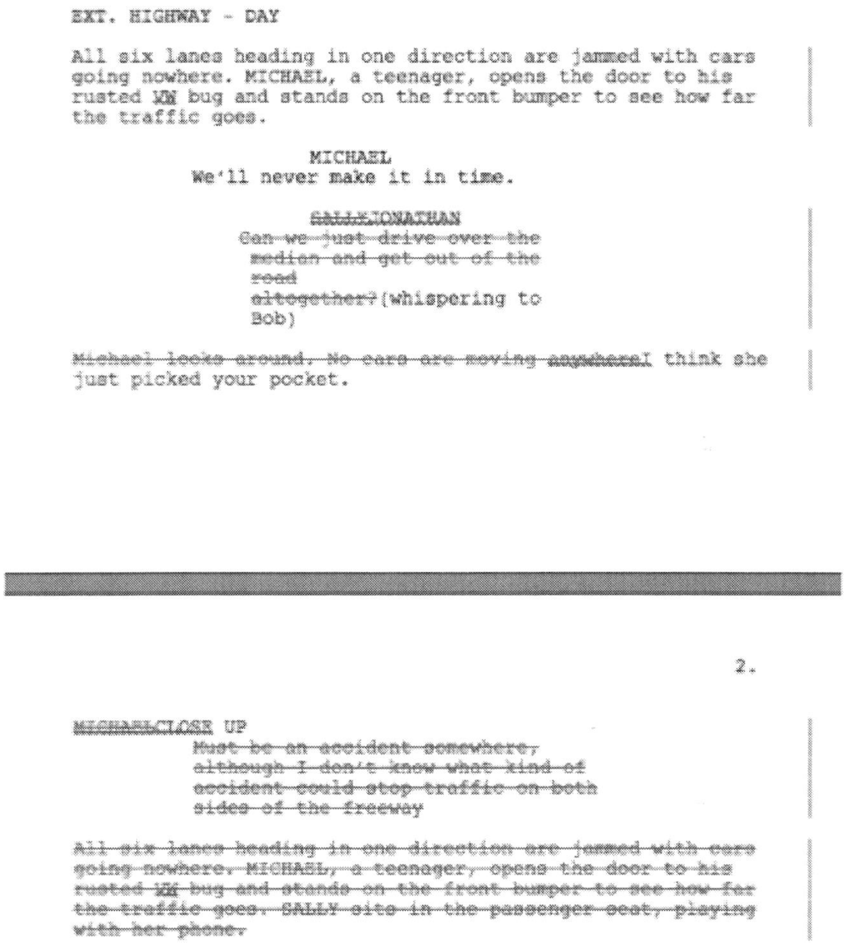

```
EXT. HIGHWAY - DAY

All six lanes heading in one direction are jammed with cars
going nowhere. MICHAEL, a teenager, opens the door to his
rusted VW bug and stands on the front bumper to see how far
the traffic goes.

                    MICHAEL
          We'll never make it in time.

                    SALLYJONATHAN
          Can we just drive over the
          median and get out of the
          road
          altogether?(whispering to
          Bob)

Michael looks around. No cars are moving anywhere.I think she
just picked your pocket.
```

                                                            2.

```
MICHAELCLOSE UP
          Must be an accident somewhere,
          although I don't know what kind of
          accident could stop traffic on both
          sides of the freeway

All six lanes heading in one direction are jammed with cars
going nowhere. MICHAEL, a teenager, opens the door to his
rusted VW bug and stands on the front bumper to see how far
the traffic goes. SALLY sits in the passenger seat, playing
with her phone.
```

Figure 12-6. Final Draft can identify differences between two versions of the same screenplay.

Summary

In this chapter, you learned how to edit your screenplay by splitting the document window in half (either vertically or horizontally) so that way you can edit one part of your screenplay while viewing a different part of that same screenplay.

You also learned how to use ScriptNotes to attach notes to specific parts of your screenplay. Think of ScriptNotes as the digital equivalent of attaching sticky notes on the pages of a screenplay.

You also learned how to mark revisions in a screenplay by manually defining revisions or letting Final Draft track those revisions automatically. If you have two versions of the same screenplay, Final Draft can show you the differences between them.

Editing and revising a screenplay is normal, so don't be surprised when it happens to your screenplay, no matter how perfect you may think it might be. In the original screenplay for "Alien," there was no android trying to sacrifice the crew to keep the alien alive as a living weapon. A second writer added those changes, which ultimately made the story stronger.

So don't be afraid of revisions. Sometimes revisions can wreck a screenplay, but often times they improve it. In either case, once you know what someone revised, you can always choose to reject or change their revisions afterwards.

Save your document by pressing Command+S (Macintosh) or Ctrl+S (Windows). In the next chapter, you'll learn how to print your screenplay in Final Draft.

13 PRINTING AND SHARING A SCREENPLAY

Once you've finished writing your screenplay and taken time to revise it, you'll eventually want to show it to others. The old fashion way of sharing screenplays meant printing and binding copies, stuffing them in envelopes, and mailing them out to others. This method still works, but it's slow and annoying. Here's the newer way of sharing a screenplay.

Since nearly everyone either uses Final Draft or a screenwriting program that can import and open Final Draft files, it's far easier just to send a Final Draft file by e-mail or on a USB Flash drive. Once someone receives your screenplay as a Final Draft file, they can edit or change that file and send it back to you.

If you want to share your screenplay with others, but don't want them to edit or change your screenplay, you can create a PDF (Portable Document Format) file. Almost every computer can open and view a PDF file using free programs like Adobe Reader. With a PDF file, you can share a screenplay and prevent anyone from making any changes. For added security, you can even password protect a PDF file.

Exercise #34: Printing a Screenplay

Despite everything going digital, sometimes you'll need a printed copy of a screenplay. You can print your whole screenplay or select pages. Remember that when you print a screenplay, anyone can make copies of that screenplay and share them with people you may not want to see your screenplay.

Filmmaker Quentin Tarantino found this out the hard way when he sent copies of his script, "The Hateful Eight," to a select number of people, but someone betrayed his trust and shared his script without his permission. To prevent this from happening, Final Draft offers a watermark feature.

Watermarks let you type descriptive text that appears printed on every page. That way you can put someone's name as a watermark and when that person receives your screenplay, their name will appear in the background. If that person now shares the screenplay, the watermark will identify where that copy came from.

Watermarks are optional, but can provide a way to track who shared a screenplay. Each time you print your screenplay, you can change the watermark. To create a watermark, follow these steps:

1. Click the **Document** menu and choose **Watermark** (Macintosh) or click the **Document** tab and click the **Watermark** icon (Windows). A Watermark dialog box appears as shown in Figure 13-1.

Figure 13-1. The Watermark dialog box.

2. Click in the **Watermark text** box and type the text you want to appear as a watermark, such as the name of the person you're sending your screenplay to read.
3. Click **OK**.

At this point, you won't see your watermark until you actually print your screenplay. To make sure your watermark appears correctly, you can save paper by doing a Print Preview instead. Print Preview shows how your printed pages will look on the screen before you print them out. Once you're happy with the way your pages look, then you can print them out.

To see a Print Preview of your screenplay as shown in Figure 13-2, do the following:

- Click the **File** menu and choose **Print Preview** (Macintosh)
- Click the **File** tab and click the **Print Preview** icon (Windows)

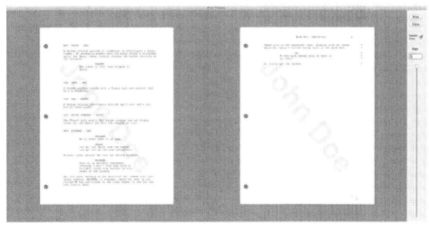

Figure 13-2. Print Preview can show you watermarks as gray text that appears diagonally across each page.

From the Print Preview screen, you can click the Print button to start printing. If you want to choose different print options, such as only printing a range of pages instead of your entire screenplay, you'll need to use the regular Print command instead by doing the following:

- Click the **File** menu and choose **Print**, or press Command+P (Macintosh)
- Click the **File** tab and click the **Print** icon, or press Ctrl+P (Windows)

When you choose the Print command, Final Draft displays a Print Script dialog box that lets you choose the printer to use, how many copies to print, whether to selectively print just revised pages, pages containing certain scenes, or pages containing one character's dialogue (known as "sides") as shown in Figure 13-3. (Macintosh users may need to click the **Show Details** button to see their full printing options.)

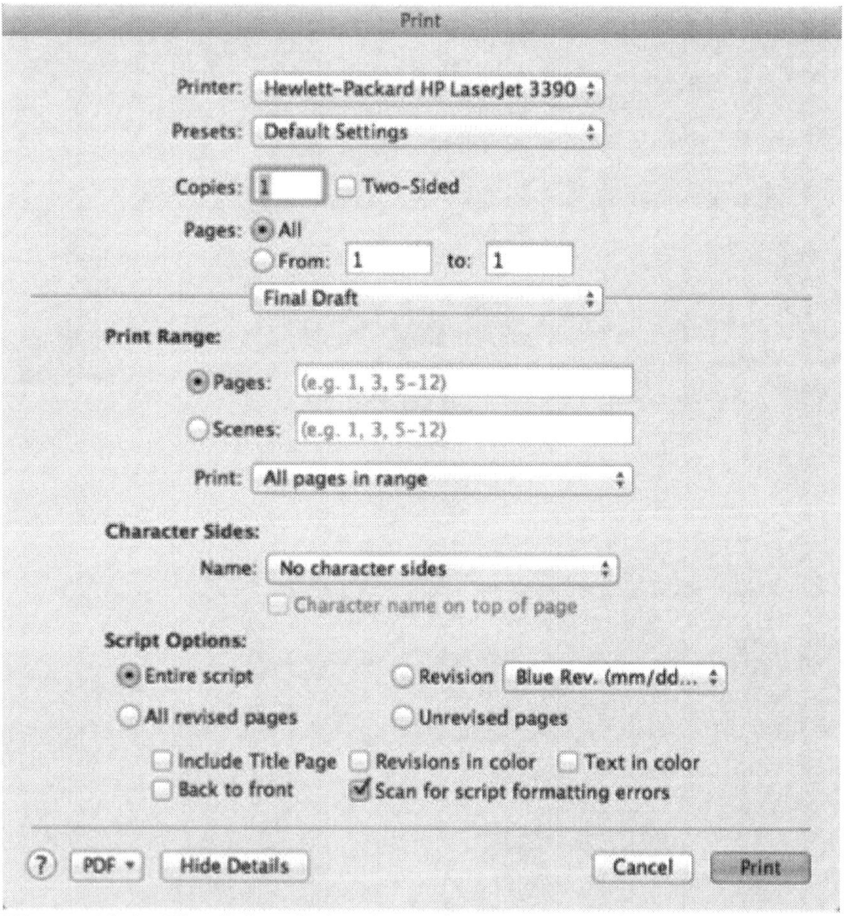

Figure 13-3. The Print dialog box gives you a variety of options for printing your screenplay.

Tip: Before you can choose to print specific scenes, you need to number them first. To have Final Draft number your scenes, click the **Production** menu and choose **Scene Numbers** (Macintosh) or click the **Production** tab and click the **Scene Numbers** icon (Windows).

For a little more control over printing, Final Draft also lets you create custom headers and footers. You can use custom headers and footers to add identifying text on each page, such as "Draft 3 - September 4, 2015."

To create a custom header or footer, follow these steps:

1. Click the **Document** menu and choose **Header and Footer** (Macintosh), or click the **Document** tab and click the **Header and Footer** icon. A Header and Footer dialog box appears with commonly used text (Page, Date, Scene, Label, Active Revision, and Collated Revisions buttons) as shown in Figure 13-4.

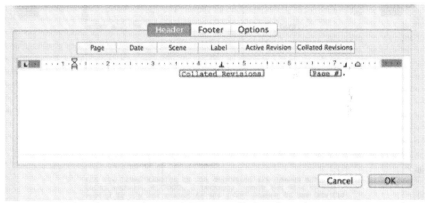

Figure 13-4. The Header and Footer dialog box lets you customize headers and footers for printing.

2. Move the cursor where you want to place text and either type text or click on a button (Page, Date, Scene, etc.) that represents the text you want to insert. (You can use the Backspace and Tab keys to modify your header.)
3. Click the **Footer** tab to edit a footer.
4. (Optional) Click the **Options** tab to define whether to print headers or footers, and which page to start printing headers and footers on as shown in Figure 13-5.

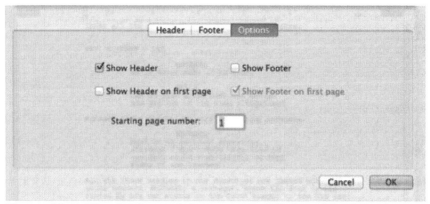

Figure 13-5. The Options tab lets you modify how Final Draft prints headers and footers.

5. Click **OK.**

Exercise #35: Sharing a Screenplay File

Wasting time and paper to print a screenplay can often be troublesome. A faster method is to share your screenplay as a digital file. Since nearly every screenplay word processor can import Final Draft files, you can just share a copy of your Final Draft file with others.

Just remember that if you share a Final Draft file, others can modify that file. If you're collaborating with others, this won't be a problem. However, if other people aren't using the latest version of Final Draft, you could run into file incompatibility issues.

To resolve this problem, Final Draft lets you export your screenplay in a variety of different file formats. Some popular file formats include:

- .fdx — This represents the latest Final Draft file format. Use this if you're sharing files with someone using Final Draft 8 or higher, or if someone's screenplay word processor knowns how to import the latest Final Draft files.
- .fdr — This represents the older Final Draft file format

from version 5 - 7. Use this if you're sharing files with someone whose screenplay word processor cannot import newer Final Draft (.fdx) files.

- .rtf — This represents Rich Text Format files, which is a universal word processor format that preserves formatting of text.
- .html — This represents HyperText Markup Language files, which are used to create web pages to display text on the Internet. Unless you want to share your screenplay as a web page, you probably won't need to use this file format if someone wants to edit your screenplay.
- .txt — This represents plain text files that even ancient computers and word processors can read. Unfortunately, .txt files lose all formatting including text indentation for character names. Only share screenplays in .txt format as a last resort because you'll wind up having to reformat everything all over again.

To export your screenplay in a different file format, follow these steps:

1. Click the **File** menu and choose **Export** (Macintosh), or click the **File** tab and click the **Export** icon (Windows). An Export dialog box appears.
2. Type a file name in the **Export as** text box (Macintosh) or the **File name** box (Windows).
3. Click on the **File Format** (Macintosh) or the **Save as type** popup menu (Windows) and choose a file format as shown in Figure 13-6.
4. (Optional) Click on a folder to store your exported file.
5. Click **Save**.

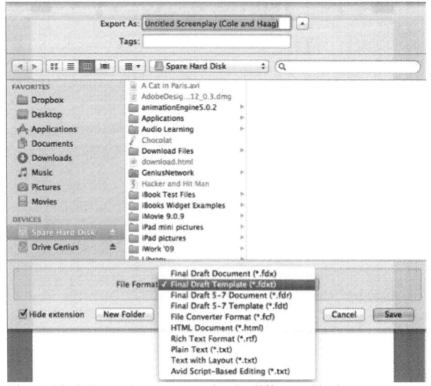

Figure 13-6. Exporting a screenplay in different file formats.

Exercise #36: Sharing a Screenplay as a PDF File

If you want someone to read your screenplay but not necessarily edit it, then you should save your screenplay as a PDF file instead. To save a file as a PDF file, do the following:

- Click the **File** menu and choose **Save As PDF** (Macintosh)
- Click the **File** tab and click the **Save As PDF** icon (Windows)

Even though PDF files can't be edited (unless the user has special PDF editing software like Adobe Acrobat Pro), someone could still share a PDF file copy of your screenplay over the Internet and you would have no idea who leaked it.

To restrict and track PDF files, consider putting a unique

watermark (see Exercise #34) on your screenplay before saving it as a PDF file. If you're using the Macintosh version of Final Draft, you can even password protect a PDF file as well.

To password protect a PDF version of your screenplay using the Macintosh version of Final Draft, follow these steps:

1. Click the **File** menu and choose **Print**, or press Command+P. A Print dialog box appears. (You may need to click the **Show Details** button to enlarge the Print dialog box.)
2. Click on the **PDF** button in the bottom left corner of the Print dialog box. A menu appears as shown in Figure 13-7.

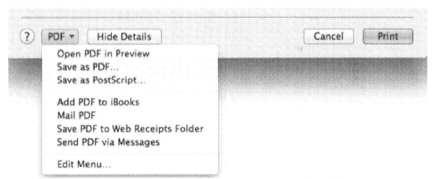

Figure 13-7. The PDF button lets you create a PDF file.

3. Choose **Save as PDF**. A Save As dialog box appears to let you type in extra information about your file, such as the author's name as shown in Figure 13-8.

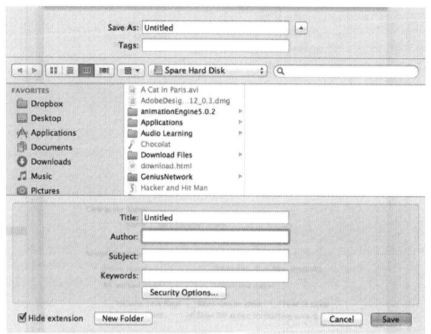

Figure 13-8. The Save As dialog box gives you additional options for storing information about your PDF file.

4. Click the **Security Options** button. A PDF Security Options dialog box appears where you can define a password to keep others from opening, printing, or copying text from your PDF file as shown in Figure 13-9. Ideally, choose a password that uniquely identifies the recipient of your screenplay, such as that person's name or phone number. The goal is to make it difficult for unauthorized users to see your screenplay and make it easy to identify where an unauthorized copy of your PDF file might have come from.

Figure 13-9. The PDF Security Options dialog box lets you password protect your file.

5. Type a password and click **OK**. The Save As dialog box appears again.
6. Type a name for your PDF file and click **Save**. Final Draft creates a password-protected PDF file.

Just as watermarks can help you track where unauthorized copies of a screenplay might have come from, so can password protection restrict who can see your screenplay. Even if someone shares the password with others, that password can identify which person originally received the PDF file.

Hackers can easily crack passwords on PDF files, but most people won't know how to do this. Combined with watermarks, passwords can insure that anyone who gets a copy of your screenplay will think twice about sharing it with others without your permission.

Exercise #37: Printing Reports

Besides printing all or part of your screenplay, Final Draft can also print reports that show you information about specific parts of your screenplay such as the following:

- Scene
- Location
- Character
- Cast
- Script
- ScriptNotes
- Statistics

A Scene report lets you see how many scenes you have, how many pages they take up, and the page numbers where they appear in your screenplay as shown in Figure 13-10.

```
UNTITLED FARMLAND - SHOOTING SCRIPT --
               SCENE REPORT

SCENE #  SCENE HEADING                              PAGE #   LENGTH

0                                                      1       1/8

1        EXT. MAST FARM - NIGHT                        1       2/8

2        EXT. MAST HOUSE - CONTINUOUS                  1        1
            DOCTOR (1), HENRY (1), WALTER (0)

3        EXT. MAST FARM - DAY                          2       2/8
            WALTER (0)
```

Figure 13-10. The information provided by a Scene report.

A Location report lets you see how many times a particular location appears in your screenplay and the page number where you can find that location used in a scene.

The Character report lets you see where a character appears and how often that character speaks in each scene as shown in Figure 13-11.

The Cast report lets you see how many times a character appears in a scene and how often he or she speaks.

The Script report lets you select which elements of your screenplay to print and which to exclude. So if you're only interested in just reading dialogue, then you can create a Script report that only shows dialogue regardless of which character says it.

The ScriptNote report lets you print out all your ScriptNotes so you can read them easily and use the report as a checklist to find and address each ScriptNote.

MY HIT SCREENPLAY -- CHARACTER REPORT FOR "MICHAEL"

SUMMARY:

MICHAEL speaks 2 times (33%) for a total of 28 words (46%).

MICHAEL appears as a non-speaking character 1 times.

MICHAEL interacts most with SALLY.

DETAIL:

Scene: INT. MOVIE THEATER - NIGHT   P.1

Non-speaking.

Scene: EXT. HIGHWAY - DAY   P.1-2

MICHAEL: We'll never make it in time.

MICHAEL: Must be an accident somewhere, although I don't know what kind of accident could stop traffic on both sides of the freeway

Figure 13-11. A Character report.

The Statistics report lets you see how many words your screenplay uses as well as showing which characters interact with others, which scenes they appear in, and how many words of dialogue they have.

When Final Draft creates a report, it creates a separate document that you need to save. To create a report, follow these steps:

1. Click the **Tools** menu and choose **Reports** (Macintosh) or click the **Tools** tab and click the **Reports** icon (Windows). A menu appears.
2. Choose the report you want such as Character Report or Statistics Report. Depending on the report you chose, Final Draft may ask you to choose various options before creating your report as a document that you can save and print separate from your screenplay.

Summary

In this chapter, you learned how to print all or part of your screenplay, and how to use watermarks to control distribution of your screenplay. You also learned how to customize headers and footers, and how to create reports to help you understand your screenplay better.

You also learned how to create PDF files and export your screenplay in a variety of file formats that you can share with others who may be using an older version of Final Draft or a different screenwriting word processor altogether.

Obviously there are plenty of other features in Final Draft that weren't covered in this book, but if you followed along with your own story ideas, you should feel comfortable using Final Draft and seeing how its various features can help you organize and write a screenplay.

Remember, the best tool in the world is useless if you don't know how to use it properly. Final Draft can take care of the mundane and tedious details of writing and organizing a screenplay. It's up to you to do the creative work to write the best screenplay possible.

As a screenwriter, keep learning from books, conferences, and watching great movies that inspire you (and bad movies that make you realize, "I could write something better than that"). There is no one best book to read or any "secret" method to writing a great screenplay other than continually honing your writing skills and getting better at writing every day.

Once you get comfortable using Final Draft on your computer, you might also want to get Final Draft Writer for an iPad. That way you can write, edit, and read your Final Draft files wherever you take your iPad.

Final Draft Writer supports all features of Final Draft 9 including ScriptNotes and General Notes. To make typing easier, Final Draft Writer includes special keys on the virtual keyboard for creating common formatting styles such as Scene headings, Character names, Dialogue, and Transitions as shown in Figure 13-12.

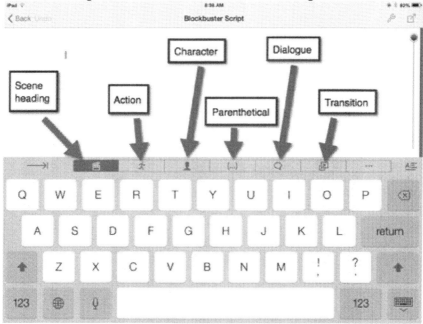

Figure 13-12. Final Draft Writer for the iPad provides special keys for formatting text.

To share files between Final Draft 9 on your computer and Final Draft Writer on your iPad, you have three choices:

- Use the File Sharing option in iTunes
- Use Dropbox (you'll need to create a free Dropbox account)
- Send files to yourself as an e-mail attachment

By using both Final Draft 9 on your computer and Final Draft Writer on your iPad, you can work on your screenplay anywhere you go.

FINAL WORDS

I hope you've found this e-book helpful and interesting to learn Final Draft and the craft of screenwriting in general. For more information on writing screenplays, I invite you to visit my screenwriting blog, www.15minutemoviemethod.com, and read my other e-book The 15-Minute Movie Method that goes into more detail about creating a screenplay using a structured approach.

If you have a dream of writing a screenplay, don't give up and don't get discouraged. Even the best screenwriters were novices once so keep learning and keep writing. Whatever happens in the future, the surest route to success will always be persistence and gradual improvement.

As Thomas Edison once said, "*Our greatest weakness lies in giving up. The most certain way to succeed is always to try just one more time.*"

You can succeed as a screenwriter. Now try one more time and prove it to the rest of the world.

37090160R00108

Made in the USA
Middletown, DE
19 November 2016